Karmic and Spiritual Astrology

A Comprehensive Exploration of Reincarnation, Karma, Zodiac Houses, Moon Phases, and Soul Connections

Your Free Gift
(only available for a limited time)

Thanks for getting this book! If you want to learn more about various spirituality topics, then join Mari Silva's community and get a free guided meditation MP3 for awakening your third eye. This guided meditation mp3 is designed to open and strengthen ones third eye so you can experience a higher state of consciousness. Simply visit the link below the image to get started.

https://spiritualityspot.com/meditation

Or, Scan the QR code!

Table of Contents

Part 1: Karmic Astrology

The Ultimate Guide to Reincarnation, Karma, Astrological Houses, Zodiac Signs, and Moon Phases

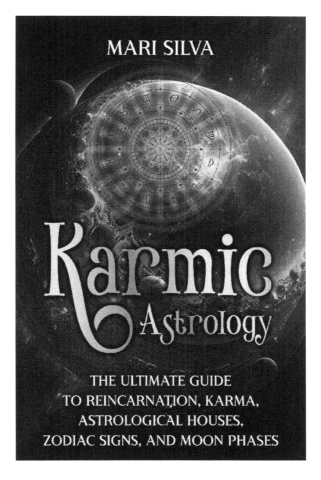

Introduction

If you look at any living being, you will notice certain patterns that all living things have. There is something common between different species and even within specific versions of each specie. The world and even the universe are made up of repetitive patterns, systems, processes, and structures. Karmic astrology is the study of the universe concerning you and how universal forces influence you. More importantly, there is a yin and yang to everything, and every action has an equal and opposite reaction, and there exists a duality in the universe. Through Karmic astrology, you will uncover things about yourself and the world around you that you may not have understood or acknowledged.

However, when discussing something as complex as human existence, its past, or even the future, it cannot be comprehended by a simple explanation. It is presented concisely and simply to the recipient, but much work must be done in the background to make understanding possible. Like how an aircraft looks quite simple when you see it, but you do not see the incredibly complex engineering that happens in the background to make this product a reality.

Similarly, karmic astrology is an interesting way of unraveling secrets about your life; however, it is not as simple as you think. Throughout this book, we will look at all the most important aspects of karmic astrology, what they mean, and how to use them to your advantage. With the knowledge shared in this book, you will evaluate your natal chart and apply this knowledge to any situation because you have the appropriate information at hand.

No part of understanding karmic astrology is more or less important than the other. Everything is important, from the birth chart reading to understanding the moon phases and astrological houses to making karmic predictions. How you apply this information to your life is what makes the difference. While you may only be interested in learning about yourself, you must see things in the bigger picture to really understand things. All nature is intertwined through the universe's fabric, so understanding any one part requires understanding the whole.

Through the information shared in this book, you will learn how to look at the bigger picture and find yourself in this sea of knowledge. Karmic astrology takes time to master, and there is a lot of room for error. The deeper your understanding is, the more you practice, and the more accurately you decipher any situation. Karmic astrology has a history spanning more than two thousand years. Over time, this science has evolved, improved, and expanded. The knowledge of karmic astrology we have at our disposal today is extremely dense and concise, so be ready to spend some time getting your head around it all.

This book is structured specifically to help people with a basic knowledge of karmic astrology or without previous knowledge. Therefore, it will benefit you immensely to go through this book chronologically. Everything is interconnected, and the book has been laid out to make it easier to understand these concepts. Also, keep in mind that these are all predictions and forecasts. Don't be surprised if real-world results vary.

Chapter 1: Karmic Astrology 101

"There is not one Astrology with a capital A. In each epoch, the astrology of the time was a reflection of the kind of order each culture saw in celestial motions, or the kind of relationship the culture formulated between heaven and earth." – Alexander Ruperti

Most people have heard of astrology. However, they often do not realize there are several branches of this discipline. Astrological traditions differ based on the part of the world you live in and what you hope to get from a session with an astrologer.

For example, people new to astrology commonly start a session with someone versed in psychological (also known as modern) astrology or who practices "traditional Western" (Hellenistic, Medieval, etc.) astrology. However, for a different perspective, you can also explore evolutionary astrology, which gives you an understanding of your current and past lives, or Vedic astrology, which is meant for people looking to incorporate astrological suggestions into their daily lives.

Astrologers often consult locational, electional, relationship, and horary astrology specialists when making key life decisions. Of course, these are only a few options available. Another popular alternative is karmic astrology.

What Is Karmic Astrology?

To properly understand what karmic astrology represents, you must first understand the meaning of the two words constituting this discipline: "Karma" and "astrology."

Karma is a concept found in many religions worldwide, and there are almost too many to name. There are many translations of the word; however, you can think about karma as your actions and the result of those actions.

Theological belief holds that a person's karma is a combination of two things: The action a person undertakes and the person who performs that action's intent. This also applies to an action that is planned but never performed—it can affect a person's overall karma as much as a successfully carried-out action can.

You create positive karma when your intentions are good or your actions are positive. If your intentions or actions are bad, your karma is negatively affected. It means that a person can do something positive, but they will still suffer bad karma if their intentions are bad. At the same time, if your intentions are positive, but your actions turn out negative, you can still create good karma for yourself.

In some schools of Hindu theology, a person's karma is inherently linked to the idea of rebirth. Therefore, a person with positive karma will have a better life at rebirth than someone with negative karma. In some schools of thought, a person who dies with negative karma will be reborn as a non-human animal, and the worse your karma, the less significant the animal you are reborn as. However, if you die with positive karma, you will be reborn as a human—the better your karma, the better your position in your next life.

In other schools of thought, having positive karma is one of the requirements for reaching emancipation or moksha—being liberated from the cycle of death and rebirth, and reaching true enlightenment instead. Additionally, Buddhism and Jainism have schools of thought that look at karma differently.

However, most schools of thought in Hinduism, Buddhism, and Jainism feature the theme of causality, essentially indicating a system of cause and effect. If an action happens, it will result in a specific, predetermined reaction.

In the case of karma, it means that a person's actions affect the lives they live, as do the intentions behind them. Specifically, karma holds that deeds, or actions, have like effects, so earning good karma will result in good effects for a person, while earning bad karma will result in bad effects.

It is not always specified what these effects will be, and they may not happen immediately. The effects of karma could appear later in a person's life or future lives. However, it's essential to note that karma is not a system of reward and punishment. Rather, it is a law resulting in consequences.

Astrology concerns how planetary bodies, such as the stars, planets, Sun, and Moon, impact human lives. This practice dates back to at least the second millennium BC and was practiced in several ancient cultures, including the Maya, Hindus, Chinese, Mesopotamians, ancient Greeks, ancient Romans, and Arabs.

As mentioned above, there are several variations of astrology, depending on which geographical tradition you follow and what you hope to learn from a session with an astrologer. In general, there are three major branches:

- **Natal Astrology:** This is the branch most people think of when they hear the word astrology. It makes predictions and analyses based on a person's birth date and time. It often involves charting the sky patterns at the exact moment of your birth (known as a natal chart) and making predictions based on this information. It can also be seen in the popular practice of zodiac-based horoscopes since these predictions are predicated on your date of birth.

- **Mundane Astrology:** This branch of astrology seeks to make predictions about larger matters beyond just a single person. For example, when making predictions about the economy, wars, and other national matters.

- **Interrogatory Astrology:** Like natal astrology, this branch generally focuses on a single person. However, natal astrology makes predictions about the course of a person's life. Interrogatory astrology is more specific, making predictions about specific issues. For example, when is the best date for a person to move home or understand the astrological basis for a specific illness or ailment?

Karmic astrology is most commonly aligned with natal astrology, sharing some similarities. One term commonly used in natal and karmic astrology is houses.

Houses is the term used when referring to a person's natal chart. Once the natal chart is made, it is divided into twelve sections. These sections are known as houses, and a different zodiac sign rules each house. Each house is also linked to a different area of your life, such as relationships, career, communication, etc.

What sign rules what house depends on your time, date, and location of birth, and the way a sign interacts with a certain house affects the analysis of your natal chart.

Understanding Karmic Astrology

Now that you understand what karma and astrology are, it is time to consider the practice of karmic astrology.

As mentioned above, karma involves believing that your actions have positive and negative effects. These effects are not seen instantaneously; some may not even be in your current lifetime but instead reveal themselves in future lives.

That is where karmic astrology comes in.

Like karma, karmic astrology believes that the circumstances of your current life result from past actions of your current life and the effects of unresolved actions in a past life. Karmic astrology offers you the chance to understand the effect of these past lives.

This branch of astrology believes that everything you do and everything that happens to you has a reason rooted in karma. Suppose you want to break your current cycle of mistakes and move forward. In that case, you must understand the karma currently affecting your life. Karmic astrology can help.

For this reason, karmic astrology is occasionally known as past life astrology. It is concerned with helping people identify the problems that have their roots in karma from a past life so they can move forward. Once you understand your current karma, you can take actions to address the issue and fix your karma if you need to.

What Does Karmic Astrology Involve?

You will learn the intricacies of karmic astrology in-depth throughout this book. However, to get you started, here is a basic understanding of what karmic astrology focuses on.

As previously mentioned, your natal chart is divided into twelve sections or houses. A karmic astrology session begins with the creation of your natal chart.

Once your astrologer has created your natal chart, the analysis starts. Karmic astrology focuses on three of the twelve houses: The 4th, 8th, and 12th—all of which are associated with the water element.

- **The Fourth House:** This is the house of your family karma. Just as your karma affects your life, so does your family's karma. This house describes the familial karma you are born under, allowing you to understand what familial habits or patterns you should alter to change your karma.

- **The Eighth House:** This is the house of your partnership karma. It represents karma from your relationships with people beyond your family. The interpretation of this house will help you understand repressed emotional issues and relationship patterns you should take a closer look at and maybe reconsider.

- **The Twelfth House:** This is the house of unredeemed and collective karma. It helps you understand the impact of subconscious service, including actions that you did not take intentionally.

The analysis of your natal chart will also look at the position of the following planetary bodies:

- **Sun:** Helps you understand your life's purpose according to your karma, including your fears, weaknesses, etc.

- **Moon:** Symbolizes a person's karmic past and unresolved issues you carry with you from your past lives mirrored in your current life. The placement of the house of the moon can show negativity in a previous life—where you failed to be as good and true as you could have been. This resulted in an unbalanced experience in that lifetime and is a concern that you will need to resolve through karmic astrology in this lifetime.

- **Saturn:** Other forms of astrology see Saturn as a negative sign and symbol of impending trouble. In karmic astrology, it serves as the judge of your karma. It symbolizes the karmic stumbling blocks you will encounter and will help you move past them. Saturn is so important in karmic astrology that it is sometimes referred to as the "lord of karma."

The two other planetary-bodied karmic astrology focuses on are Rahu and Ketu. These are bodies unique to Hindu texts. Rahu is a shadow entity, considered the entity that causes eclipses and rules meteors. Ketu is considered to be a shadow planet.

In Western astrology, they are known as the north and south lunar nodes. These points show the orbit of the Moon and Earth around the Sun.

- **Rahu/North node:** Rahu represents your karmic path and helps identify your karmic goal or life mission. This goal represents new beginnings and is one that you cannot rely on in your past lives and experiences.

- **Ketu/South node:** Ketu represents your karmic roots and ancestry. It is, essentially, an Achilles heel and serves as a symbol of past issues and karma you want to resolve through your karmic astrology session. It may not necessarily be negative (karma is not necessarily negative), but it is something you need to overcome to move forward and focus on living your present life.

Karmic Astrology, Karmic Debt, and Karmic Relationships

A detailed karmic astrology reading can help you in many ways. One of the primary reasons people seek out these readings is to understand their karmic debt.

Karmic debt is essentially debt you accrued in your past life. It is negative karma you created in a previous life, which you still have to experience. It is something you still have to pay off or debt from a past life.

It's essential to note that karmic debt does not mean a major catastrophe. You can address this debt in various ways and move forward. Once your astrologer has identified any karmic debt you may have, they will also help you move past it.

Another issue many people have in mind when visiting a karmic astrologer is karmic relationships.

Karmic relationships involve two partners in a relationship and their respective karmas. As you now understand, each partner brings their own karma into a relationship and is linked through their karma. From this, we can deduce that those involved previously must use current relationships to learn who they are and how they must act.

A reading focusing on a karmic relationship involves resolving the karmic problem tying the two people together by removing negative karma from one or both partners. These relationships usually fizzle out once the karma linking the two halves is resolved.

It's important to note that the people in a karmic relationship need not be romantically involved. It can be any relationship, including a friend, coworker, parent, or even a pet.

How Good Is Your Karma?

So, you are interested in exploring karmic astrology further, but you're unsure where your karma stands at the moment. If you're wondering how good your karma is, this quiz is for you.

Simply answer each question truthfully, and tally your results based on the instructions at the end of the quiz.

1. You find a wallet abandoned on the train. You decide to:

    a)   Find the owner.

    b)   Leave it where it is—someone will come and get it soon.

    c)   Take out some money and return the wallet.

    d)   Keep it for yourself.

2. Do you talk to homeless people?

    a)   I would if I needed to.

    b)   Perhaps a "hi" as I walk past.

    c)   I'd feel a bit nervous doing so.

    d)   Never.

3. You do someone a favor. Do you:

    a)   Let it stay a secret—you're doing it for them, not for the acknowledgment.

    b)   Let them know, but downplay your efforts—you'd like a little acknowledgment but aren't interested in being the center of attention.

    c)   Ensure you let the person you helped know—after all, you did it, so they should be aware that you liked them.

    d)   Make sure the person you helped knows—you want to ensure they know to pay you back in the future.

4. You encounter a lost and confused tourist on the street. You:

    a)   Walk with them to their destination.

    b)   Offer to help with directions.

c) Ignore them and power walk past.

d) Point and laugh at their predicament with your friends.

5. Do you return books from the library on time?

a) I return them early more often than not.

b) I generally return them on time, but I have been late on occasion.

c) I try returning them on time, but it's hard, and I'm generally late.

d) I can't remember the last time I returned a library book after checking it out.

6. Do you volunteer?

a) As much as I can.

b) Occasionally, but I don't have much time to spare.

c) I've considered it but have decided against it.

d) Never—I have limited time and need to focus on making money.

7. Do you recycle?

a) Always.

b) As much as possible—although I do slack off occasionally.

c) When it's convenient.

d) Never.

8. Your best friend is going through a significant breakup. Do you:

a) Hang out with them, be there for them, and listen to them for as long as possible.

b) Spend some time with them and take them out for a meal or two.

c) Take them out a couple of times.

d) Offer to split a round of drinks.

9. Would you agree to work at a company whose mission you morally disagreed with in return for a significant salary?

a) No.

b) I would consider it, but I'd need a lot more information.

c) I'd donate some of my paychecks, but yes.

d) Yes.

10. **Do you think people should judge others based on a single action?**

a) No.

b) Depends on the action in question.

c) I think judging others on their actions is justified.

d) Yes—an illegal act should always be given the full book, regardless of personal situations.

Once you have done the quiz, tally your responses. Count how many of each option you got—how many a's, b's, and so on. Determine which choice has the highest number.

Those with the highest number of a's have the best karma, while those with tons of d's need to do a little work to increase their positive karma. Those with more b's and c's have a mix of good and bad karma. If you have more b's, you lean toward positive karma, while those with more c's lean toward negative karma.

Now that you know your karma, the next step is to precisely understand how this affects your karmic astrology reading. The next chapters will cover this, helping you understand how to read your birth chart, explore the importance of zodiac signs and elements, and explain planets, retrogrades, moon phases, and nodes. The chapters will also help you align your life with your karmic life purpose and more.

If you've been curious about your karma and its role in your past and future, you are in the right place. This book about karmic astrology will ensure you know everything important there is to know about this branch of astrology to focus on using it to improve your life and the lives of those around you. All you need to do is turn the page and keep reading as the next chapter helps you to understand how to read your birth chart and explains why it is important.

Chapter 2: Reading Your Birth Chart

You have probably heard of horoscopes more than once in your life. For years, people have used astrological patterns to predict various characteristics of a person. These include personality, mood, luck, fortune, future, and many others. Birth charts are also commonly known as natal charts or, in simpler terms, horoscopes. These charts help you gain tremendous insight into your inner self and psyche.

Birth chart.
https://pxhere.com/en/photo/682841

Understanding Your Birth Chart

A birth chart is a map of where planets are at the moment of a person's birth, situation, relationship, or journey. Specifically, a person's birth chart predicts their individual personality and the key events of their life. A birth chart utilizes constellations and planetary positions to establish an insightful astrological blueprint and provides a roadmap to making good life decisions. Birth charts help reveal the following characteristics of your life:

- Behavioral patterns, healthy and toxic
- Your strengths and weak points
- Relationship compatibility
- Karmic lessons

To read your specific birth chart, you need to know your birth date, time, and place. It is preferable to get the exact time. However, since this information is not always available, use a rough estimate to read your birth chart. The usual layout of a Western birth chart consists of three wheels or circles equally divided into twelve sections, equating to the twelve houses. These three wheels consist of three main components that must be observed. These include the twelve houses, ten planets residing in the twelve houses, and the twelve zodiac signs. Below is what a generic birth chart looks like:

The Inner Wheel

The inner circle represents the location or exact coordinates of your birthplace. It is scientifically proven that the Earth revolves around the Sun instead of the opposite way around. However, astrology focuses on the solar system's interaction with Earth. We can see that the Sun moves around our planet and passes through each sign for around thirty days.

The Mid Wheel

The mid-wheel consists of twelve sections representing the twelve astrological houses. Each section presides over a specific area of your life, including relationships, careers, wealth, luck, etc. The houses start from the ascendant, located in the middle left of your circle, and will move counterclockwise. It is also important to note the position of the ascendant to identify the twelve houses.

Observe a horizontal line that goes through the inner circle to the outer circle. To the left will be your ascendant, or the rising sun representing

---

your worldly personality. This is the personality you use to interact with the rest of the world, and it determines things like your style, looks, temperament, self-esteem, etc. Located to the right is the descendant representing your personality in various relationships, romantic or otherwise.

Next, observe the vertical line, or meridian, which cuts through the middle of the horizontal line. At the bottom, the meridian is the Imum Coeli representing the inner persona of an individual. This part helps identify the person's emotional roots, soul memories, and how they behave privately. Finally, the Midheaven or Medium Coeli is located at the top of the meridian. It embodies your public persona, helping you identify your career path and ambitions and how you can fulfill them to reach your true potential.

The Twelve Sections

The twelve sections consist of the twelve houses, as explained before. These planets exist within different houses, which offers valuable insight into your personality and how you interact with the world. These houses provide a roadmap to understanding your past, present, and future. As the planets move within these regions, different events and changes (physical and mental) occur.

To interpret your birth chart, you first need to observe the locations of the planets in each house. Interestingly, a house can have multiple planets while other houses are empty. So, do not get confused, as it is perfectly normal for the planets and stars to cluster together at the time of someone's birth. The empty houses do not mean there is any deficiency. However, the presence of multiple planets in a house calls for extensive interpretation.

You need to understand the functions of each planet and house to do this and then connect them with the zodiac signs for a complete picture.

The Outer Wheel

As an important concept that arranges the twelve signs of the zodiac—all of which are named after groups of stars—the outer wheel consists of the zodiac signs named after star constellations. Each sign consists of an individual quality or personality. These traits are what distinguish the zodiac signs from one another. These signs will coincide with different houses and create the final interpretation of your birth chart. Here is a simple list of the zodiac signs and their personality traits.

Zodiac Sign	Ruling Planet	Dates	Glyph	Traits
Aries	Mars	20 March - 19 April	♈	Pioneer, Warrior, Daring
Taurus	Venus	20 April - 20 May	♉	Builder, Manifestor
Gemini	Mercury	21 May - 21 June	♊	Networker, Communicator
Cancer	Moon	22 June - 22 July	♋	Nurturer, Motherly
Leo	Sun	23 July - 22 Aug	♌	Performer, Leader
Virgo	Mercury	23 Aug - 22 Sept	♍	Healer, Server, Humble
Libra	Venus	23 Sept - 23 Oct	♎	Diplomat, Delegator
Scorpio	Pluto, Mars	24 Oct - 21 Nov	♏	Psychologist, Transformer
Sagittarius	Jupiter	22 Nov - 21 Dec	♐	Explorer, Philosopher
Capricorn	Saturn	22 Dec - 19 Jan	♑	Timely, Purposeful
Aquarius	Uranus, Saturn	20 Jan - 18 Feb	♒	Reformer, Humanitarian
Pisces	Neptune, Jupiter	19 Feb - 20 March	♓	Dreamer, Compassionate

The Planets

We focus on a total of ten planets when reading the birth chart. Each is located in different houses, depending on your date and place of birth. The energy of these planets influences our lives significantly. However, truly what we do with these energies ultimately decides our fate. Among these planets are the two luminaries, the Sun, and the Moon. Then, we have Mars, Venus, Jupiter, Saturn, Mercury, Uranus, Neptune, and Pluto. These planets are classified into:

Planet	Glyph	Zodiac Sign	House	Description
Sun	☉	Leo	5th	Unique identity, creative potential
Moon	☽	Cancer	4th	Emotions, nurturing feelings
Mercury	☿	Gemini, Virgo	3rd and 6th	Communication, rational thoughts
Mars	♂	Aries, Scorpio	1st and 8th	Motivation, energetic, sexuality
Venus	♀	Taurus, Libra	2nd and 7th	Beauty and art, love, and relationships
Jupiter	♃	Sagittarius, Pisces	9th and 12th	Philosophical, search for answers
Saturn	♄	Capricorn, Aquarius	10th and 11th	Karmic lessons, time restrictions
Uranus	♅	Aquarius	11th	Rebellious, revolutionary feelings
Neptune	♆	Pisces	12th	Change, spiritual awakening

| Pluto | ♇ | Scorpio | 8th | Transformation, regeneration, destruction |

The Twelve Houses

The twelve houses each represent an aspect of your life and need to be understood in detail. We will delve deeper into the twelve houses in the upcoming chapters. For now, you can get the gist of what each house stands for from this table.

House	Governs	Characteristics
1st House	Self	Appearance, Outward Personality
2nd House	Possessions	Money, Possessions, Values, Skills
3rd House	Communication	Mental Thought Process, Communication, Siblings
4rth House	Family and Home	Home, Parents, Roots, Inner Security
5th House	Pleasure	Romance, Children, Creativity, Fun
6th House	Health	Work, Health, Self-Improvement
7th House	Partnerships	Marriage and Other Relationships
8th House	Sex	Sex, Death, Regeneration, Sharing
9th House	Philosophy	Higher Education, Philosophy, Religion, Travel, Law

10th House	Social Status	Career, Status, Reputation, Vocational Purpose
11th House	Friendships	Friends, Groups, Goals, Aspirations
12th House	Subconscious	Solitude, Transcendance, Institutions, Self-Sabotage

How to Interpret Your Birth Chart

Once you have learned about the various zodiac signs, planets, and houses, it is time to interpret your birth chart First, generate your birth chart using an online source, or draw it up if you are an expert. Next, consider the zodiac sign and house each planet is in. Do not try to read all the planets at once. First, narrow down on a single planet and identify the house it is present in and its associated zodiac sign. Once you've done this, list and interpret them according to the following functions:

Planets — Represent what drives you, what you enjoy

Houses — Represent where you should expect growth or change

Zodiacs — Represent the manner of accomplishing a task

For instance, let us assume your birth chart has Uranus in Aries, in the fourth house. List that down and refer back to the tables and data you've learned above. From that, we can conclude:

Planet — Uranus (Ability to learn, grow, revolutionize)

House — Fourth House (Home and family)

Zodiac — Aries (passionate, ambitious, strong)

From this information, we can interpret that you're very passionate about your family and home, and you learn and grow mostly through your loved ones. Your emotional well-being is mainly connected with your roots, so your happiness depends on your family.

Exercise: Try Interpreting;

Here is an example birth chart to try your hand at interpreting the different meanings and insights.

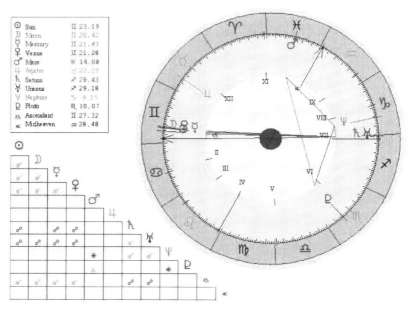

Birth chart and their interpretations.
https://commons.wikimedia.org/wiki/File:Birth_chart_example.JPG

1st House

Planet _____

House _____

Zodiac _____

Interpretation

_____
_____
_____
_____

Planet _____

House _____

Zodiac _____

Interpretation

_____
_____
_____
_____

2nd House

Planet _____
House _____
Zodiac _____
Interpretation

_____
_____
_____
_____

4th House

Planet _____
House _____
Zodiac _____
Interpretation

_____
_____
_____
_____

Planet _____
House _____
Zodiac _____
Interpretation

_____
_____
_____
_____

8th House

Planet _____
House _____
Zodiac _____

Interpretation

_____
_____
_____
_____

Planet _____
House _____
Zodiac _____
Interpretation

_____
_____
_____
_____

9th House

Planet _____
House _____
Zodiac _____
Interpretation

_____
_____
_____
_____

10th House

Planet _____
House _____
Zodiac _____
Interpretation

_____
_____
_____
_____

11th House

Planet _____
House _____
Zodiac _____

Interpretation

_____
_____
_____
_____

12th House

    Planet _____

    House _____

    Zodiac _____

    Interpretation

_____
_____
_____
_____

For You: Worksheets

Now, generate birth charts and use the following worksheets to interpret your birth chart or your friends' and loved ones' charts.

1st House

    Planet _____

    House _____

    Zodiac _____

Interpretation

_____
_____
_____
_____

    Planet _____

    House _____

    Zodiac _____

    Interpretation

_____
_____
_____
_____

2nd House

Planet _____

House _____

Zodiac _____

Interpretation

_____

_____

_____

_____

Planet _____

House _____

Zodiac _____

Interpretation

_____

_____

_____

_____

3rd House

Planet _____

House _____

Zodiac _____

Interpretation

_____

_____

_____

_____

Planet _____

House _____

Zodiac _____

Interpretation

_____

_____

_____

_____

4th House

Planet _____

House _____

Zodiac _____

Interpretation

_____

_____

_____

_____

Planet _____

House _____

Zodiac _____

Interpretation

_____

_____

_____

_____

5th House

Planet _____

House _____

Zodiac _____

Interpretation

_____

_____

_____

_____

Planet _____

House _____

Zodiac _____

Interpretation

_____

_____

_____

_____

6th House

Planet _____

House _____

Zodiac _____

Interpretation

_____

_____

_____

_____

Planet _____

House _____

Zodiac _____

Interpretation

_____

_____

_____

_____

7th House

Planet _____

House _____

Zodiac _____

Interpretation

_____

_____

_____

_____

Planet _____

House _____

Zodiac _____

Interpretation

_____

_____

_____

_____

8th House

Planet _____

House _____

Zodiac _____

Interpretation

_____

_____

_____

_____

Planet _____

House _____

Zodiac _____

Interpretation

_____

_____

_____

_____

9th House

Planet _____

House _____

Zodiac _____

Interpretation

_____

_____

_____

_____

Planet _____

House _____

Zodiac _____

Interpretation

_____

_____

_____

_____

10th House

Planet _____

House _____

Zodiac _____

Interpretation

_____

_____

_____

_____

Planet _____

House _____

Zodiac _____

Interpretation

_____

_____

_____

_____

11th House

Planet _____

House _____

Zodiac _____

Interpretation

_____

_____

_____

_____

Planet _____

House _____

Zodiac _____

Interpretation

_____

_____

_____

_____

12th House

Planet _____

House _____

Zodiac _____

Interpretation

_____

_____

_____

_____

Planet _____

House _____

Zodiac _____

Interpretation

_____

_____

_____

_____

KEY

(For interpretation of the first and last planet in the exercise birth chart)

Rising Sign (28 Degrees Sagittarius)

Even though you can be infamous for your indiscretion and bluntness, you are actually quite open, honest, and outgoing. No one should take anything you say personally because you mean no harm. Living your life in a straightforward manner is highly appreciated, but you consider social niceties an obstacle to true communication. You possess lots of energy and will become restless if restricted. You enjoy freedom as opposed to being anxious and feeling trapped. You enjoy the outdoors, where you can express your freedom and energy, and so you enjoy sports and socializing, and you will liven up any gathering.

Planet 1 — Mars (ambitious, courageous, energetic)

House — First House (self-esteem, unique identity)

Zodiac — Capricorn (purposeful, timely)

Interpretation: Extremely ambitious, you are willing to work very hard to reach your goals. You're very practical, cautious, and conservative. You require concrete results for all your effort, and you manage to excel in whatever you set your mind to. You own a great sense of responsibility and self-discipline. However, make sure not to judge others.

Planet 11 — Pluto (transformation, rebirth, regeneration)

House — Twelfth House (subconscious, transcendence)

Zodiac — Sagittarius (explorer, philosopher)

Interpretation: Society's cherished beliefs and totems will be radically changed for your entire generation. Many traditional concepts will be entirely altered, if not destroyed completely. The rights of individuals to pursue their own course in life will be reasserted.

Rising Sign (Sagittarius)

This is a person with an open personality, known for their frankness and honesty. However, they can be, at times, blunt and insensitive, which usually offends people. People close to this person have learned not to take everything they say personally because of their indiscreet nature. This person appreciates the simplicities in life and considers social formalities and niceties barriers to real and effective communication. Therefore, this person would rather be straightforward and simple than opt for a formal approach to a conversation.

This person has lots of pent-up energy and, if not dissipated in some way, can become restless and feel confined. Furthermore, this person loves the outdoors and demands freedom, whether freedom of speech or to do as they like. Their lack of conforming to social niceties does not make them any less of a social person; their lively spirit and enthusiasm make them very popular in social gatherings.

First House

Planet — Mars (ambitious, courageous, energetic)

House — First House (self-esteem, unique identity)

Zodiac — Capricorn (purposeful, timely)

Interpretation: The ruling planet is Mars, and this person is extremely ambitious about their goals and aims. They will do anything necessary to achieve their set goals. The zodiac Capricorn adds a trait of purposefulness to their personality. This person is very practical about their goals and demands tangible results within time limits. Their unique identity is very responsible, they are dedicated to their goals, and have a keen sense of self-discipline that lets them succeed in their tasks. However, this person tends to judge others by their status and prestige and always looks at others as competition.

Planet — Neptune (change-loving, spiritually awakened)

House — First House (self-esteem, unique identity)

Zodiac — Aquarius (reformer, humanitarian)

Interpretation: As a reformer, who loves to bring change, this person will idealize the ability to analyze any given situation objectively. They will work on many humanitarian causes to cure society of its many flaws and injustices taking place every day. However, they will have to be very careful when working toward change and for the rights of individuals amid a fast-changing society.

Second House

Planet — Uranus (rebellious, revolutionary)

House — Second House (money, possessions, values, skills)

Zodiac — Aquarius (reformer, humanitarian)

Interpretation: A reformer at heart, this person likes to bring about positive changes all around them. Whether it is for their friends, peers, or society in general, positive change drives this person. They are willing to devote their time, effort, money, skills, and energy to a purpose. However, due to their humanitarian personality, they can often end up neglecting their personal relationships.

Fourth House

Planet — Jupiter (philosophical, in search of answers)

House — Fourth House (home, parents, roots)

Zodiac — Aries (pioneer, warrior)

Interpretation: This person is well known for being an uncompromising individualist who grows and develops philosophically and needs to explore their hidden talents and abilities. Focused primarily on their roots and family, they are pioneers and warriors when fighting for their families. They take pride in their accomplishments. However, they can become self-centered and sometimes ignore the needs of the people around them.

Planet — Saturn (karmic lessons, time limitations)

House — Fourth House (home, parents, roots)

Zodiac — Taurus (builder, manifester)

Interpretation: With a builder's personality, this person needs proper order in their life and to feel stable and secure. While they want to see change around them, they are not entirely open to adapting to new and unpredictable situations. They often experience karmic lessons and learn from them every time. However, their constant fear of the unknown makes them seem withdrawn and anxious. So, it's important that they surround themselves with supportive people to become more emotionally stable and self-supporting.

Eighth House

Planet — North node

House — Eighth House (sex, death, regeneration, sharing)

Zodiac — Leo (performer, leader)

Interpretation: Considered a natural leader, this person does not shy away from the opportunity to lead others toward completing their goals. They enjoy organizing and delegating group activities. Due to their enthusiastic and strong personality, others listen when they give suggestions and actually implement them in their work. Unlike most leaders, they are not patronizing or overly domineering in their interactions. This person also has a big, attention-grabbing personality and enjoys being in the spotlight whenever there is a large gathering. People usually love this person as long as they do not become arrogant or self-centered.

Planet — Moon (emotions, nurturing feelings)

House — Eighth House (sex, death, regeneration, sharing)

Zodiac — Virgo (healer, server, humble)

Interpretation: This person is seriously minded and cheerful at the same time. They have a stellar sense of humor, an enthusiastic personality, and a focused mind. They prefer tasks that can help them stay engaged mentally and physically. This person is considered a careful worker and will go out of their way to help others without ever being snobby about it. Their most prominent traits include practicality, reliability, efficiency, and enthusiasm. They are sometimes considered a prude but entirely devoted and caring to those they love.

Ninth House

Planet — Venus (beauty and art, love, and relationships)

House — Ninth House (higher education, philosophy, religion, travel, law)

Zodiac — Virgo (healer, server, humble)

Interpretation: This person expresses their love and affection by serving people selflessly. They often doubt their self-worth and have low self-esteem issues in relationships. This should be avoided, and they must learn to love themselves—just as they are—and then pursue other relationships. Their standards of love and perfection are very high, and they are often attracted to people based on a sense of duty or responsibility instead of genuine interest. Furthermore, they can sometimes be superficial about themselves and others, which leads to them alienating anyone they start to get close to.

Tenth House

Planet — Sun (unique identity, creative potential)

House — Tenth House (career, status, reputation, vocational purpose)

Zodiac — Scorpio (psychologist, transformer)

Interpretation: While they prefer a straightforward approach to life, this person is actually very complex and intense by nature. Their emotions in critical situations are very strong. However, they find it very difficult to express their emotions in detail and rather opt for a simplistic approach. This person might be social and popular but needs alone time to recharge and process their emotions in peace. They are usually calm and collected but become completely unforgiving when angered. They have a ton of creative potential and are very serious about their careers. They are known to be willful, tenacious, and passionate about their careers and reputations.

Eleventh House

Planet — Mercury (communication, rational thoughts)

House — Eleventh House (friends, groups, goals, aspirations)

Zodiac — Sagittarius (explorer, philosopher)

Interpretation: They have an explorative, curious, and inquisitive mind and are always looking for rational answers and logical explanations. They are interested in broad subject matters, whether philosophy, science, or religion. Their aspirations lie in abstract details associated with any subject, and they usually focus on small details.

Twelfth House

Planet — Pluto (transformation, regeneration, destruction)

House — Twelfth House (solitude, transcendence, institutions, self-Sabotage)

Zodiac — Sagittarius (explorer, philosopher)

Interpretation: When working toward change and transformation, they will see their efforts successfully regenerating society's cherished beliefs and radically changing fundamental concepts. They will reassert individuals' rights to pursue their own course in life and explore different philosophies.

Chapter 3: Zodiac Signs and Elements

The term zodiac in astronomy or astrology defines a band in the sky that the Sun, Moon, and other planets pass through, as seen from Earth. The zodiac consists of various constellations, and the Sun or other celestial bodies move through these constellations with time. The ancient Greeks and Romans divided these constellations into zodiacs and believed the position of the celestial bodies could predict future events. This gave rise to the concept of astronomical zodiacs and their associated meanings.

The zodiac symbols.
https://pxhere.com/en/photo/1001293

Every individual is assigned a zodiac sign based on the constellation the Sun was in when they were born. Astronomers believe these zodiac signs predict a lot about a person, from their likes and dislikes to their personality and possibly even some aspects of their future. As discussed in the previous chapter, these predictions are made by a birth chart. In addition, it is important to learn about the different zodiac signs and what they convey about a person. This chapter will detail the twelve zodiac signs, what elements they are associated with, and the qualities of each sign.

Zodiac Signs

1. Aries

People with Aries as their zodiac sign are often ambitious, motivated, and headstrong. This fierceness is due to Mars as the governing planet for this zodiac sign. Both witty and humorous, Aries people are good with social networks and persuasive to almost everyone around them. Although they get mad easily, it is also easy to calm them down. They will start any project with full zest and motivation but often find themselves scattered and diverted.

Aries personalities have positive and negative sides. Aries have strong personalities, not easily discouraged by minor setbacks. They have a unique zest for living and show an active and energetic spirit. However, they can be callous and insensitive when communicating in a conflicting situation.

2. Taurus

A dominating feature of this sign is their strength and strong will. The associated planet, Venus, further makes these individuals emotional. Stubborn and unwilling to change, Taurus people are somewhat rigid. However, their empathetic nature makes them worth the trouble. Logic and reasoning will not affect them much, but emotions and feelings more easily persuade them.

Taurus people are opportunists, so they go along with whatever comes their way instead of finding opportunities, which often limits their success. However, when they have money, they are very generous with it, especially with friends and loved ones. The positive side of Taurus is that they are honest and forthright in all their dealings because of their empathic nature. However, they often find it hard to trust people completely and are suspicious of everyone around them.

3. Gemini

In contrast to the previous zodiac, Gemini's key characteristic is adaptability and flexibility. The readiness to change in Geminis is indeed remarkable, which helps them make instantaneous decisions. The governing planet, Mercury, makes this trait in Geminis even stronger, resulting in an act-now-explain-later approach. This approach often comes in handy in tricky situations in the workplace or field. Geminis are imaginative, generous, and humble to those around them.

Their frequent need for change makes it impossible for existing conditions to satisfy them. The positive side of Geminis is observed in their quick wit, open-mindedness, and intellectual nature. Creativity and innovation stem naturally in their minds. However, due to the ever-changing nature of their ideas, they often do multiple things at once and end up getting side-tracked and finishing nothing.

4. Cancer

This sign's ruling planet is the Moon, and just like it, the zodiac is associated with shifting tides and personality changes. These individuals cling to traditions and culture but keep up with changing times. This contradicting nature can be associated with the fluid nature of the Moon. Cancers love to stick with their family and spend time in the comfort of their homes, yet they also love to travel to new places. People with this zodiac are highly sensitive but do not show it to people around them. They hate arguments and would rather avoid conflict than face it. They are also not great at receiving criticism and often take it to heart.

The perk of being highly sensitive is that they are extremely compassionate to the people around them. They cannot bear to see others get hurt, especially because of them. Cancers are often resigned to fate when they can't take hardships anymore. They will hide in their shells and lack the initiative to do things requiring them to go out of their way. This trait especially hinders their road to success.

5. Leo

Leos have powerful, dominating personalities and are considered born leaders. The governing planet is the Sun, which gives Leos the light to shine brilliantly. Leos are ambitious and idealistic, making them susceptible to the failure of their shortcomings. They are high-minded and intellectual. However, they are also often high-handed, resulting in overconfident mistakes.

Their impulsive nature makes them easy targets for small failures in daily tasks, but they are brave enough to stand back up and try again. Their magnetic attitude attracts people, and their charming personalities easily win them over. Leos are optimistic, energetic, and generous. You will never see a Leo being stingy when treating others. However, they can be a bit arrogant about their position and power and often mistreat others. Egocentricity is a common trait among Leos.

6. Virgo

Virgos are analyzers of deep and interesting subjects and are often the most intellectual minds of all the zodiacs. The ruling planet, Mercury, makes their decisions more impulsive, which is often a weakness for their capable minds. Their persuasive skills are among the best, convincing even the most stubborn people. Their inquiring minds don't let them rest until they have all the answers they seek.

They are good at analyzing a situation by extracting information from people and making accurate assumptions about any missing information to create a clear picture. Unlike other zodiacs, Virgos are consistent with their work and always finish their tasks to near perfection. However, this quality also brings out some bad qualities in their personality. They think their work is superior to others and are sometimes too critical of colleagues.

7. Libra

Libras are extra nice and make just decisions regarding their friendships and relationships. They try to keep everything in balance and promote goodwill, peace, and friendships, even if they have to go out of their way to do so. Their ruling planet, Venus, makes them attracted to beauty and art. Their sympathetic nature makes it impossible for them to say no to a friend or family member in need. They would even stick up for a stranger if they thought they were being mistreated.

Their intuition is especially strong, which helps them sniff out any deceit or misinformation others may present. However, in their quest to make everything right and balanced, they are often insincere and lie to prevent any relationship imbalance. It could mean they give in easily in arguments even if they know they are right so as not to escalate the situation any further.

8. Scorpio

Scorpios are fearless individuals, confident in themselves, and guided by their self-control and boldness. Their ruling planet, Mars, only adds to the fuel of the already passionate Scorpios and gives them the will to face any challenges and obstacles that might come their way. Scorpios are secretive, sensitive, and very observant. However, once they're roused to take action, nothing can stand in the way of their success.

When they work for others, they rise very high, but they can often become domineering and aggressive, resulting in their ultimate downfall. It is their greatest weakness. Scorpios are natural fighters if the opportunity presents itself. However, they can act hypersensitive in many situations and boast about themselves to deal with neglect from their loved ones. Another weakness is that they have no hold over their temper and are easily angered.

9. Sagittarius

Sagittarius individuals are hard workers and give their best when working on a project. However, they have trouble concentrating on projects of immediate importance. From their governing planet, Jupiter, they get a happy, cheerful, and vibrant personality that combines with their zest and hard work for the perfect score. However, Sagittarius people often overwork themselves and struggle with anxiety throughout their projects. Therefore, they should focus primarily on rewarding projects that make their struggles worthwhile. Sagittarians are the most friendly and easygoing people of all zodiacs. A great weakness of Sagittarians is their financial mismanagement. They are often attracted to gambling and other vices.

10. Capricorn

This sign produces deep, philosophical thinkers and scholars. Their intellect also helps them apply their knowledge to practical life. When working on a specific thing, they will be deliberate and calm. Unlike many impulsive zodiac signs, Capricorns exhibit a drive and passion for knowledge but approach it in a scholarly fashion. Capricorns tend to be loners and prefer solitude to complete their tasks. However, this trait leaves them feeling lonely sometimes. They are charitable, generous, and humble to people deserving of help. To friends, Capricorns are the most loyal and trustworthy of all zodiacs. Sometimes, they may also act too bossy and drive people away. They can also be excessively critical of others and offend people when working together.

11. Aquarius

Aquarius zodiacs are mostly devoted to humanitarian causes and look toward making life easier for people. They take on great missions to help people and have a friendly attitude, making them comfortable to be friends with. Their governing planet, Saturn, provides them with the energy and willpower needed to complete their tasks with quiet determination. They are loners, too, but unlike Capricorns, Aquarius people do not mind company when they get it.

Aquarius people are very tolerant and considerate, making them quite popular. Yet they still prefer working in solitude to focus on the task at hand completely. Aquarius people are dreamers but can get carried away by their dreams and seem rather eccentric to others. They don't like admitting their faults and mistakes, resulting in fanatic views.

12. Pisces

Pisces people are the most unassuming bunch of the whole zodiac. They are so humble that they fail to give themselves credit even when they're knowledgeable about certain things and let others take the credit. The governing planet, Jupiter, endows these individuals with an extremely generous nature that they let others walk all over them. They fail to snatch opportunities and let others take the spotlight in these circumstances.

The humbler they are, the more they doubt their abilities. This ultimately results in worry and anxiety. Pisces people are the most cautious of all the zodiac and will think multiple times before they take a leap. The philosophical nature of this zodiac often results in individuals being talented in music, art, or other creative activities. However, Pisces people miss out on good opportunities and become depressed and gloomy about life because of their cautious attitude.

Elements

The zodiacs are further understood by two main factors that classify them into certain categories. These include elements and qualities. Elements speak to the fundamental nature of a sign, whereas qualities are concerned with how the signs express themselves. Air, Earth, Fire, and Water were implemented by the ancient Greeks as the building blocks for the universe and everything within it. Each zodiac sign is associated with one of these four elements. These elements describe the basic nature of an individual's persona. To properly understand zodiac signs, we must understand what these elements represent.

1. Earth

Virgo, Taurus, and Capricorn are all earth signs. Anyone linked to these signs is generally a secure and stable person, grounded in reality.

They are not much for taking risks and avoiding conflict. The earth element represents building or creating things, so earth zodiacs desire to create or build things in their lives. Whether these are solid, physical, or strong emotional aspects, earth elementals are all about stability.

It can be as simple as creating comfortable rooms in a home or creating jobs or opportunities for others. Zodiacs with the earth element are influenced to accumulate worldly possessions around them for a sense of stability. However, this trait can turn into an unhealthy habit when individuals become greedy or materialistic.

The earth element represents a sense of duty and responsibility, and zodiacs associated with the earth element feel a need to help and support people around them. Earth elementals are logical and take a measured approach that guarantees little to no risk. However, these people are so focused on the outcome that they sometimes overlook other people's feelings. In short, zodiacs supported by earth have their feet on the ground and their eyes on the prize.

2. Air

Libra, Gemini, and Aquarius are all air signs. The zodiacs graced by this element have the added benefit of intellect. These individuals are smart thinkers and can reason abstractly. Their intellect is coupled with their creative mind to bring forth critical thinkers. Air sign zodiacs are all about communicating their thoughts and ideas to the world.

They analyze things deeply and can be pretty useful in a dilemma. Air signs are neither too feisty nor too calm. Depending on their mood, they can have a calm and collected attitude like a fresh breeze but can be easily angered like the howling wind. Air signs are humane and often look toward helping others as much as they can. With their objective thinking and cooperative nature, no issue is too difficult for them to solve.

3. Water

Associated with Cancer, Scorpio, and Pisces, water represents the fluid nature of these zodiacs. Water is fluid, wavering, and flowing, and so are the qualities of these zodiacs. Water zodiacs have a higher sense of intuition and feel everything at a much higher intensity than others. These signs are emotional and nurturing and often act on emotions rather than logic.

Water signs are very compassionate to others, feel their problems as their own, and will seek solutions for them. Those supported by water are all about beautiful and aesthetic things, whether art, music, or nature.

They desire beauty and want others to be happy because of this beauty. Much like water, these zodiacs, if stagnant, can lose their way and become self-indulgent.

4. Fire

Sagittarius, Aries, and Leo are all fire signs. As expected, the zodiacs graced by fire are indeed ferocious. These signs are passionate, ambitious, and never lacking in courage. However, just like fire, it becomes very difficult to contain them if they get out of control. The fire element gives these zodiacs lively spirits and a well of creativity. The people graced by the fire element are self-confident, spontaneous, and have a tremendous zest for life. These signs are the most passionate in a love match.

Qualities

The quality of a zodiac defines an individual's attitude to life and how they approach projects and different tasks. The qualities are explained below:

1. Cardinal

Cancer, Aries, Capricorn, and Libra have cardinal qualities. These signs are the initiators of the zodiac, plus they are located at the jumping-off points on the chart wheel of birth charts. Aries is placed at the ascendant, and so on. Signs with a cardinal quality want to get things started. They are ambitious, quick, and active. Cardinals start many projects but fail to complete them successfully because signs with this quality are more interested in starting things than finishing them. Cardinal energy can sometimes seem overbearing, but this drive helps them complete many tasks.

2. Fixed

Fixed qualities are associated with Scorpio, Taurus, Leo, and Aquarius. These individuals prefer steadiness over pace. They will work on their projects calmly and collectedly and get them to completion. These individuals are determined to complete their tasks and have a stable approach to problem-solving. Fixed quality signs are highly self-reliant and never doubt themselves as they move steadily toward their goals. On the flip side, these signs can be rigid and stubborn to changing environments.

3. Mutable

Virgo, Pisces, Gemini, and Sagittarius are mutable signs that are more flexible in their approach to life. These individuals are willing to change their behavior, approach, and expressions depending on the circumstances. They are highly resourceful and well-liked by others because of their flexible personalities. They have a strong sixth sense that helps them scope out possible opportunities and shape them in ways that help the most. However, their desire to please everyone is the same one that gets them into trouble.

Here is an easy-to-understand chart summarizing the learnings and understandings of zodiac signs and their characteristics.

Zodiac Sign	Ruling Planet	Symbol	Glyph	Quality	Element
Aries	Mars	Ram	♈	Cardinal	Fire
Taurus	Venus	Bull	♉	Fixed	Earth
Gemini	Mercury	Twins	♊	Mutable	Air
Cancer	Moon	Crab	♋	Cardinal	Water
Leo	Sun	Lion	♌	Fixed	Fire
Virgo	Mercury	Virgin	♍	Mutable	Earth
Libra	Venus	Scales	♎	Cardinal	Air
Scorpio	Pluto, Mars	Scorpion	♏	Fixed	Water
Sagittarius	Jupiter	Archer	♐	Mutable	Fire
Capricorn	Saturn	Sea goat	♑	Cardinal	Earth

Aquarius	Uranus, Saturn	Water bearer	♒	Fixed	Air
Pisces	Neptune, Jupiter	Fish	♓	Mutable	Water

The development of zodiacs has a rich history in astronomy. While it started by associating individuals with their birth zodiac sign, modern astrology considers all twelve zodiacs. It combines these with the twelve houses and the position of the planets on each occasion. This combined information gives us a much clearer picture of our horoscope than a simple zodiac prediction. Each zodiac sign is ruled by single or multiple planets that significantly impact their characteristics. Similarly, each of the qualities and elements impacts how a certain zodiac's traits and characteristics are shaped. Thus, each factor has a unique significance when interpreting someone's zodiac signs or natal chart readings.

Chapter 4: Planets and Retrogrades

The Earth is surrounded by two luminary bodies, the Sun, the Moon, and eight planets. Each body carries a profound amount of energy specific to it. These planetary energies affect you on every level.

It is not only their energy that influences your life but also their movements. These bodies revolve around the Sun and cross paths with the twelve zodiac signs of the universe. Every zodiac sign carries its energy, so when a planetary body meets a zodiac sign, it creates a different energy field affecting your life.

This chapter will teach you about the planets' movements and pace. You will also learn how these seemingly subtle movements influence your life in space.

Pace

In astrology, planets are divided into two groups, inner and outer planets. Inner planets move much quicker than outer planets, meaning you feel their effects more than you would feel the movement of outer planets.

As the planets go around the natal chart, they create aspects. Aspects are certain angles created by the planets. These angles are an expression of the energy that two planets create together.

Inner Planets

☉ Sun

This luminary body moves one degree every day in your natal chart. It means it remains in the same zodiac sign for thirty days and takes 360 days to return to the same degree as your natal sun. Due to its fast pace, aspects created by the Sun last for three days.

The Sun represents your core personality and ego. It is important that you understand that it only reflects who you are at heart, but it's not an expression of who you are as a complex being. It represents your masculine side, along with your charisma, confidence, and creativity.

When the Sun moves around, you start questioning your identity. The feelings this movement might inspire in you solely depend on its aspects. Harsh aspects can make you dissatisfied with yourself, while soft aspects create a harmonious environment.

☾ Moon

On average, the Moon travels to the next sign within two to two and a half days. It means that the Moon takes twenty-eight days to complete its cycle around the chart. Its aspects last for three hours.

The Moon is your emotions and represents your feminine side. It includes your intuition, softness, vulnerabilities, and nurturing side.

Your emotions are entirely vulnerable to the movements of the Moon. You will experience emotional fluctuation whenever the Moon travels to a different sign or has aspects with other planets.

☿ Mercury

Mercury spends about three weeks in one sign and completes its cycle after 88 days. Usually, the aspects it creates last for approximately two days.

This planet represents your mind, including communication skills and style, cognitive and intellectual abilities, perception, and thought patterns. It is mostly responsible for the conscious side of your brain and relates more to logic than the abstract. Mercury also represents short travels, affecting things like vehicles and various transportation means.

Depending on the planet's newly found location, you might experience mental fluctuations—experiences on the road or with your car. It can affect your traveling, especially the journey on your way there.

♀ Venus

Venus usually stations for eighteen days in one sign when traveling around the signs and then moves on. It takes 224.5 days to complete its cycle, and its aspects last for two days.

Venus is the planet of relationships, love, life, beauty, and finances. The planet rules all relationships and is not limited to romance. It is also associated with art, possessions, social life, sensuality, and pleasure.

Relationships and other Venusian life aspects might undergo periodic shifts with the planet's movements and aspects. However, even if you are experiencing a harsh aspect, it will only last a few days.

♂ Mars

Mars spends around two months in one sign and twenty-two months to cover the whole natal chart. Its aspects last for approximately a week.

This planet rules physical activities, sexual energy, force, aggression, animalistic behavior, bravery, and desire. It is also connected to weaponry, violence, war, and accidents.

Mars's effects are usually felt because of its strong impact. So, when it moves, you may find yourself in situations that come out of nowhere. They could be forceful and disruptive to your daily routine.

Depending on its placement and aspects, you may find yourself in a fight you did not initiate or become aggravated easily and feel anger surging through your veins without a specific reason.

♃ Jupiter

Jupiter lingers for a whole year under one sign, meaning it completes its journey every twelve years. The aspects it creates usually last for three weeks.

Jupiter is known as the planet of good fortune. It also rules long-distance traveling, philosophy, the abstract mind, philosophy, religion, indulgence, leisure, luck, growth, and prosperity.

There is usually nothing to worry about with this planet's movement because it will bring you good fortune wherever it may be. However, the only factor that could dull your good luck is the difficult aspects of Jupiter.

Outer Planets

♄ Saturn

Saturn spends two and a half years in each sign and takes twenty-nine and a half years to reach its natal placement. The aspects it creates last for six weeks on average.

Known as the teacher, Saturn rules discipline, order, ambition, responsibility, tradition, and patience. It causes limitations and restrictions to teach you about something that you lack.

This planet is somewhat feared because it may take blessings away from your life. However, this only lasts for a short time. You will be immune to its effects once you have learned your lessons.

♅ Uranus

Uranus spends seven years in each sign and takes around 84 years to land in its natal placement. Its aspects last for three months.

This planet is associated with originality, eccentricity, rebelliousness, innovation, technology, magic, psychology, and astrology. It causes sudden changes and disruption. It is concerned with humanitarian issues and is futuristic within itself. Naturally, it affects humanitarian causes and supports innovative and futuristic ideas.

This planet's effects are often unexpected because they depend on what house it is in and its aspects with other planets. So, check your transit Uranus to know what changes you might experience during the seven years.

♆ Neptune

Neptune stays fourteen years in each sign and takes 164 to complete a full cycle around the natal chart. Its aspects last for two years on average.

This planet rules the water bodies, art, music, spirituality, illusions, dreams, subconscious, drugs, drug abuse, hypnosis, sleepwalking, and trances.

Generally, Neptune's effects are not immediately felt. It will take some time to settle into a sign, and then it creates certain themes in your life for fourteen years. You can learn about your Neptunian effects by studying the sign it is currently in.

♇ Pluto

Pluto stays in each sign anywhere from fourteen to thirty years. It might take around 248 years to complete its cycle around your birth chart. Its aspects may last several weeks, but it depends on its speed in your chart.

Pluto is an intense planet. It rules anything hidden, death, rebirth, transformation, obsessions, phobias, beginnings, endings, and isolation. It also rules dark things like coercion, kidnappings, viruses, and bacteria.

Typically, Pluto is perceived as the planet of transformation. So, wherever it is in your natal chart, it transforms you based on its current placement. You must study its current sign and compare it to your natal Pluto to interpret this planet's effects correctly.

Planets in Retrograde

Now that you have an idea about the planets' movements, it is time to learn about planetary retrogrades. Retrograde is a planetary movement where the planets appear to be moving backward for a certain period and then return to their normal pattern.

The planets do not move backward. The Earth just moves faster than the planet's orbit. So, the planet seems like it is moving backward.

Mercury

Mercury retrograde. Even if you are unfamiliar with astrology, you have probably heard of this term somewhere. This phenomenon happens approximately three times a year and usually lasts three weeks.

There are a few advantages and disadvantages to this periodic movement. During this time, you might feel nostalgic. You may be thinking about your favorite things from childhood or entertaining your nostalgia and experiencing fond moments.

Another advantage is reconnecting with people. This planet rules communication, so it makes sense that when it is in retrograde, you reconnect with the friends you have lost touch with.

One of the disadvantages you could deal with during this time is technology and transportation issues. It's also rather easy to create conflict during this period because there is much room for communication.

You should be mindful of your communication and ensure you understand people correctly to avoid misunderstandings.

Astrologists warn against signing contracts because your cognitive abilities are usually slightly clouded.

Venus

Venus goes into retrograde approximately every eighteen months and lasts about forty days. This planet is closest to Earth, so its effects are significantly powerful. Its retrograde digs up repressed relationship issues and brings them to the surface.

Discussing relationship issues could be considered a disadvantage, but Venus wants you to heal and experience healthier relationships, so it helps you by bringing them up.

You could also come face-to-face with your physical insecurities, which are unpleasant to experience and deal with.

However, the positive side of a Venus Retrograde is healing. Although it is uncomfortable, acceptance, awareness, and healing are your tools during this rough time.

As strong as the urge to run away from your problems, you must be compassionate and brave enough to take this journey head-on. So, avoid running away and begin your healing journey during this time.

Mars

Mars goes into retrograde every twenty-six months and lasts 80 days, meaning that you do not experience it as often as other planetary retrogrades. You experience stagnancy in your sex life, and your energy levels drop significantly. The retrograde may bring up pent-up anger, so you could be angrier than usual during this period.

The best way to deal with Mars retrograde is to find healthy ways to deal with suppressed anger.

It is probably best to avoid acting on impulse or entertaining your aggression. It may be best to sit back, reflect on your feelings, and take time off from starting new projects or setting things into motion. It's time to relax now.

Jupiter

This planet goes retrograde every nine months and remains in this position for approximately four months. During this time, you are more introspective and philosophical. You are most likely to question everything around you. You will look closely at laws, rules, religions, and beliefs instilled within you and never questioned before.

One of the distinctions of this time is that it shakes your blind faith and provokes you to question it. This may be a difficult thing to go through, but Jupiter pushes you to connect with your higher mind and spiritual self.

It may be best to avoid resistance against the planet and open yourself to the universe.

Freeing yourself from false beliefs and exercising self-discipline is encouraged because the retrograde might make you want to self-indulge unhealthily.

Saturn

Saturn retrogrades once every year and stays that way for four and a half months. This time of year is challenging, and you will be learning to face your inner critic. It is tough because inner critics are harsh and difficult to please. You will feel more restricted during this time and face fear-based limitations.

Nobody likes to feel limited, but you must endure this disadvantageous factor of this period. On the other hand, you will come out of this period with more realistic expectations of yourself. You could be more disciplined and patient with yourself after the retrograde is over.

Running away from responsibilities and giving into fear-based limitations are not encouraged during this time.

A better course of action would be coming to terms with your limitations as a human and learning the lesson the planet teaches.

Saturn's lessons are based on the house, sign, and aspects in your natal chart. So, check your birth chart to understand which areas need improvement in your life.

Uranus

Uranus retrogrades every year and stays in this motion for five months. This retrograde may slip the rug from under you—just when things are all right, suddenly, your world is hit by an earthquake. It is a wake-up call reminding your authentic self of the one you may have been repressing.

It may put you in difficult situations to make you confront truths you have been avoiding. As unpleasant as this is, you will need to get out of these situations by sticking to your truth and doing what is best for you.

If the planet pushes you to be yourself, it may put you in situations where your real self is repressed, and you cannot live authentically. Whatever your situation, you'll need to find a way to handle this sudden change with a clear head.

This planet will attempt to free you from the shackles of tradition and old-fashioned thinking and your inauthentic parts. So, during this time, avoid holding onto the safety of the norm and throw yourself into the unknown. The planet will bless you with good outcomes if you let go and trust that you'll be okay.

Neptune

Neptune retrogrades once a year and stays in this phase for approximately six months. Normally, this planet shields you from harsh realities, meaning that when it retrogrades, the veil drops.

This experience can be difficult because you deal with hidden feelings, thoughts, and impulses. A different side of you will rise to the surface, and you will not like it. The planet strips away your denial, and you must face your reality.

The only real benefit of Neptune retrograde is that you deal with undealt realities, whether they are yours or they surround you.

Denial can be very tempting this time of year, but it is vital that you resist this urge. If you resist Neptune's influence, it may severely force you to see the truth. So, it's best to come to terms with your truth.

You may also find yourself attracted to drug use during the retrograde. Enjoying a glass of wine is harmless, but using alcohol to escape is not encouraged during this time. Neptune rules alcohol use, so if you use it to escape, Neptune will ensure the truth follows you until you have dealt with it.

Pluto

Pluto retrogrades once a year and remains in retrograde for five or six months. As mentioned before, Pluto rules everything hidden. So, during its retrograde, you will face things hidden from you or have your secrets exposed.

You may experience disturbing memories or feelings your subconscious has protected you from. They may come to you in dreams, or you may remember them suddenly, but it will not be pleasant either way.

Transformation is needed; however, it can be painful. Unfortunately, Pluto's transformations break you or shatter your whole world. This can be a challenging time, but you should remember that you will soon meet your new, more evolved self. The thought alone can be comforting when life gets dark.

During this time, avoid resisting your transformation. The smart thing to do is to embrace it. Accepting this time of your life can help you be more self-compassionate and go through this period with as much grace as you can.

Observing planetary movements is critical to understanding the current phase you are living in. Sometimes you will find yourself in weird circumstances and do not know why or how you ended up in these situations. Normally, when you question your life because suddenly things feel off, it is most likely caused by planetary movements asking you to make necessary changes.

Chapter 5: Moon Phases and Nodes

The Moon is a powerful celestial body. It mainly harnesses female energy; however, it is not that simple. Every month, the Moon goes through nine different phases, each with a certain energy that affects you differently.

In this chapter, you will learn about the phases in detail and be introduced to their nodes.

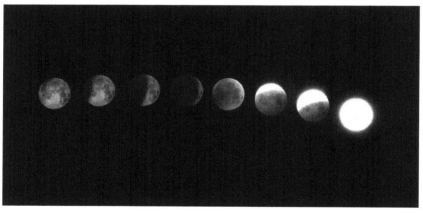

The phases of the moon.
https://www.pexels.com/photo/phases-of-the-moon-1983032/

The Lunar Phases

New Moon

The new moon is the first lunar phase in the cycle. You see it right after the dark moon when this luminary body disappears completely. It looks like a tiny sliver of the Moon, which makes sense because it is right when the Moon is between the Earth and the Sun, so, normally, you do not see much of it.

New moon.

This moon symbolizes new beginnings, new chapters, enthusiasm, energy, and motivation, and this phrase carries a lot of energy. It may end a horrible phase in your life, give you some motivation, or bless you with a burst of energy you lack.

You can harness this phase's energy in various ways. For instance, if you have wanted to embark on a project, whether in your personal life or work, now is the time to do so. You can reflect on your life during this time. Ask yourself: What path should I be taking now? Is it time I introduce myself to something new? Should I be exploring a new chapter in my life?

Waxing Crescent

The waxing crescent is the second moon phase and comes two days after the new moon. From its name, you can already tell it looks like a bright silver crescent in the night sky. This is when you see how bright the moon is after two phases of providing little or no light.

Waxing crescent.
Luisalvaz, CC BY-SA 4.0 <https://creativecommons.org/licenses/by-sa/4.0>, via Wikimedia Commons https://commons.wikimedia.org/wiki/File:Waxing_crescent_moon.jpg

The waxing crescent symbolizes courage, new opportunities, faith, positivity, and new challenges. It does not influence reckless or impulsive behavior but encourages you to take leaps of trust without overthinking things. It does not want you to be discouraged, so it gives you a little bravery and trust.

During this time, it is ideal for working on your trust. Reflect on the areas you think you lack trust in and face them. Allow yourself to be influenced by the energies the moon offers you. Be braver and speak up. What you have to say is important, and whatever new opportunities come your way now should be considered. Avoid dismissing them out of anxiety and fear. Believe in yourself and the universe.

First Quarter Moon

The first quarter moon is the third phase. It appears a week after the new moon. It looks like a half-bright moon in the sky, which is why it is occasionally referred to as the half-moon.

First quarter moon.

If half of the Moon is bright and clear, the other one is dark and hidden—similar to a binary relationship between what you can and cannot see. Therefore, this phase symbolizes strength, focus, commitment, determination, decisive decision-making, and re-evaluation. It could also represent what we can't see, whether inside us or the things beyond us.

At this time of the month, you should thoroughly reevaluate yourself. You can journal your findings to make this process easier. Think about how you have been treating yourself and others. Are you working on your goals one step at a time? Are you avoiding making goals because of fear? Reevaluate the people whom you give your time, energy, and love. Are they worth it? What do they do in return? Commit to enhancing yourself during this time, shed the fear of the unknown, and do not let it hinder your journey.

Gibbous Moon

The gibbous moon comes after the first quarter and right before the full moon, which is an interesting placement. This moon looks like a bright ball in the sky, yet you can't see it all yet.

Gibbous moon.

As mentioned, this phase is interesting because it is right before the full moon. So, why is this important? It means that it encourages you to rise to your full potential. It symbolizes development, self-worth, wealth, gains, and manifestation.

During this phase, you can manifest what you want in your life, whether a certain lifestyle, friends, situation, money, or anything else on your mind. After this, you can start thinking about how to develop these areas. If financial security has been troubling you lately, put more effort into finding a passive income or begin an easy side job because the Moon will bless you with gaining whatever you lack during this time.

Also, think about how you can reach your full potential. You may need to work on some skills or discover new things about yourself. You could read more and gain more knowledge. Use the Moon's bright illumination and enlighten your mind with knowledge.

Full Moon

The full moon is the mid-point of the lunar phases. This is as bright as the Moon is going to get. It comes right after the gibbous moon and is not difficult to identify. It is full and bright—so bright that it lights up the whole sky.

Full moon.
Gregory H. Revera, CC BY-SA 3.0 <https://creativecommons.org/licenses/by-sa/3.0>, via Wikimedia Commons https://commons.wikimedia.org/wiki/File:FullMoon2010.jpg

This phase symbolizes abundance, fertility, blooming, emotional times, powerful energy, and healing. This moon is known as one of the most powerful moons. It provides you with ample illumination and enlightenment. Suddenly, everything is clear to you, and understanding or navigating your emotions is no longer difficult.

You may be emotional during this time. Embrace it; do not run away from it. The Moon, after all, rules emotions, so when it is full, it shines a light on your emotions. You can reflect on how you feel and write it down. Think about it or talk about it with your therapist if needed. You may be facing difficult emotions during this time if you are one to run away or hide from them.

Aside from your feelings, you can work on your gratitude. The more grateful you are, the more blessings you will receive from the universe. It is the perfect timing for this since the Moon is providing you with abundance.

Waning Gibbous

The waning moon comes after the full moon when the phases parallel each other. It looks like the gibbous moon, except the shadowy side is on the other side of the gibbous moon.

Waning gibbous moon.

Remember, every phase of the full moon will be about getting rid of something or ending a chapter. When we are approaching the full moon, we are gaining and developing. However, as we move away from it, we start shedding things to begin a new cycle.

This phase symbolizes getting rid of wasteful habits or the things that bring you grief or hinder your progress. This could also be applied to unhealthy thinking or destructive habits, like self-sabotage.

Consider reflecting on the traits or habits you need to shed during this time. Things that you have been unconsciously entertaining. You need to be aware that these things do not serve you anymore, so it is time you get rid of them.

Third-Quarter

The third quarter moon comes after the waning gibbous. It resembles the first quarter moon. When you look up at the sky, you see less and less of the Moon as the cycle comes to an end.

This phase also has a shadow side. Hence, the third quarter symbolizes working on the shadow self. The shadow self contains traits you do not like about yourself, such as things you do that bring you down and do not build you up. By paying attention to this part of yourself, you can eliminate certain toxic traits or behaviors to become a better you.

Shadow work is a big aspect of spirituality. You can learn about this part of you by locating Black Moon Lilith's placement in your natal chart and understanding how it affects you and those around you. Shadow work is not an easy journey to embark on, but it is necessary for self-development.

Waning Crescent

The waning crescent moon appears after the third quarter. Again, it looks like the waxing crescent moon.

This phase symbolizes detachment and isolation. These might be difficult energies; however, they are necessary for your well-being. Staying connected to the world all the time is draining, especially if you have yet to pay attention to your energy levels. Spending time with yourself can reveal many things that need your attention. They could be anything from your feelings, unaddressed thoughts, and self-care.

During this phase, you might tell your friends you will take some time for yourself. Sit with yourself after work, take yourself out on a date, or indulge in any activity you enjoy. You can journal or take notes from a self-help book. There are no rules you need to follow as long as you spend time with yourself and avoid self-neglect.

Dark Moon

The dark moon is the final Moon in the lunar phase. It appears two days before the new moon. You cannot see it because it is barely there. It's almost like it has disappeared from the sky.

This phase symbolizes endings, wisdom, birth, rebirth, secrets, transformation, the release of inner trauma and pain, stillness, and death. Of course, events like death, birth, and rebirth are not literal with this moon phase. They represent the inner cycle you go through when you transform. The old you die, and the new you are rebirthed.

Reflect on the shadow work you have done previously and start shedding the old you during this phase. Going through a transformation phase can be difficult, so be compassionate with yourself throughout this difficult period. Exercise self-love during this time because recognizing your shadow self does not mean you are worthless or not worthy of love.

You may be experiencing fear because you feel you are losing parts of yourself—this is normal. You're losing parts of yourself, but they are those that you need to shed to gain a healthier you.

The Lunar Nodes

The Moon's nodes, also known as the north and south nodes, are two points of intersection around the Moon's orbit when it crosses the eclectic. These nodes play a vital role in Karmic Astrology. Simply, the nodes tell a story of your past life. Both carry information about your karma during this life based on how you led your past life.

Understand that the nodes go hand in hand. You cannot understand the meaning of one without the other. Together they form a complete picture, so you need to understand their positions and meaning together.

☊ North Node

The north node symbolizes the soul's growth. There are things that you lacked or did not experience in your past life. So, your karma in this life is to experience them and grow.

It points to a certain path you will be on during this life, so you must know your north node's location and meaning.

This path is full of rewards for you; however, it may be challenging to go through, like anything in life. So, when you understand what your path is, you will receive divine assistance promised by the north node placement.

Once you understand what you should be doing to reach the apex of success, you must work on yourself. Surely, this path was tailored for you the moment you were birthed. Yet, it was also made for the version of you that is willing to work on itself and has enough self-love and dedication to reach its potential.

The path that is being pointed to may not seem like you. It might point to a direction you did not imagine or never thought of as a possibility. These thoughts and feelings are normal, but trust that the universe has your best interest at heart.

☋ South Node

The south node represents your past, the foundation on which your current life is built. Certain habits and comfort zones within you are from your past lives. You can find yourself reverting to your old ways unconsciously in this life.

Aspects of the south node are important. For example, if you have a conjunction between a planet and the south node, it is time you completely moved on from your past.

You do not need to go through past life regressions or entertain past life memories because they hold no value now.

The south node can tell you a lot about your past life's karma in Karmic Astrology. You can find out about your karmic debt here.

The south node is not a crystal clear picture of who you were. Rather it is a collection of the place you grew up, your struggles, skills, and everything else about you. Through this information, you can learn about your good and bad karma.

Lunar Nodes Placements

To better understand the node's placements, look at this example of breaking down this placement.

The nodes are opposite to each other, naturally. If the north node is in the first house, the south node is in the seventh house.

Per Karmic Astrology, the north node in the first house and the south node in the seventh house means you prioritize your partner and other people close to you more than you prioritize yourself. You give them too much, and there is not enough left for you.

It also means that you feel worthless without a partner. Somehow, you think your partner completes you or is a key element to your survival. This placement says you have made many sacrifices to please your partner and others close to you.

With this placement, the north node is what you need to develop; this is the path you should be on. Developing these traits will free you from your south node karma.

Do not be surprised if you relate to your south node placement. These feelings can still arise in your current life.

☊	1st house	• Develop a healthy sense of self. • Be independent. • Work on healthy boundaries. • Avoid codependent relationships. • Build a strong identity. • Be more self-assured. • Stand up for yourself. • Learn to listen to yourself and don't put too much emphasis on what people have to say or think about you. • Prioritize yourself. • Work on self-love. • Work on abandonment issues. • Address your loneliness and find the root cause.
☋	7th house	• Feelings of worthlessness and inadequacy. • Feeling that you are not enough. • Struggled with self-love and thought you were not worthy of love, kindness, or anyone's attention. • Threatened when someone close leaves your life. • Easily fall into codependent relationships.

Identify the nodes in your birth chart.

Now, it is your turn to decode the nodes' placements.

Follow these steps for an easy interpretation:

1. **Identify their location.**

   Sign and house.

2. **Interpret the lunar node placement based on its location.**

   An easy way is to understand the properties of the sign and house with the nodes.

Understanding your emotions can be a complex and overwhelming task to complete. However, on a more positive note, studying your moon placement, the moon phase you were born under, and how it affects you can give you much insight. The present moon phase also affects your emotions, so observe how you feel under each phase every month to come closer to understanding human emotion's complexities.

You may additionally dedicate some time to studying your nodes to learn about your past and future in this lifetime.

Chapter 6: Astrological Houses

Now that you are familiar with birth charts, the zodiac, planets, and the Moon phases, this chapter explains the twelve astrological houses by listing each house and how you look at your birth chart. Lastly, it provides sign rules to explain to which house each zodiac sign belongs.

Understanding the Houses in Astrology

The birth chart consists of twelve equal sections comprising the houses. These houses differ from the zodiac wheel determined by the Sun's annual rotation. The houses reflect a twenty-four-hour rotation of the Earth around its axis, and the two systems are often combined when astrologers read a birth chart. Make sure you discover the exact time of your birth when you are creating your chart, as the slightest change will make a difference.

The houses in the astrology chart are crucial since they represent different aspects of your life based on your birth location and time. When you plot your chart, these can indicate any challenges you will face or have faced, along with the advantages you have in life.

Do not worry when you first study your chart. If you have some empty areas while others are populated with symbols, that is totally normal. Look first at your ascendant sign, as this is your starting point. Look to the left-most point on your horizon line for the sign that comes from it and applies to your birth.

When you look at the houses, start at the point marked 1 or AC and from the mid-left part of the zodiac wheel. Work anticlockwise on the chart from the first house to the twelfth house. The following are the descriptions of each house that will help you understand how the houses lying in specific signs influence your life.

First House/Ascendant/AC/Rising Sign

The first house, also known as the birth chart ruler, determines how other people perceive or see you. In other words, it is a reflection of yourself to the world. It's the side of yourself that other people view. You must know that the Sun is your sign.

Second House

The second house represents personal wealth, material goods, and self-confidence. It specifically rules everything that involves your financial standing, including liquid assets. It also expresses your feelings toward those assets. The feelings we have for material things drive our motivations when spending money. The second house also shows the career you should follow for good material gains.

Third House

The third house is about communication and how we relate to our siblings, early education, and other aspects like local travel. It determines how you interact with others in different aspects of your life.

Fourth House/Imum Coeli/"Bottom of the Sky"

This area on the chart focuses on things that happen behind the scenes in homes. Some aspects like personal views, traditions, family, and ancestors are personal, and many people don't want to share them with others.

Fifth House

This house depicts elements like casual love affairs, creativity, flirtations, crushes, fun, risks, and entertainment. It guides you in love matters.

Sixth House

The house is about personal health, household pets, daily routine, and coworkers. It is concerned with the things you encounter every day. Often, individuals who belong to this house display a high degree of organization and tend to focus on time management.

Seventh House/Descendent/DC

This house refers to current friends, enemies, and ex-partners. This is part of the area that reflects all relationships and partnerships.

Eighth House

This is a home of transformation, intuition, debt, growth, and power. It is known as the house of sex, death, taboos, and other people's possessions. The house rules other people's money and different possessions. It's also the darkest in the natal chart since it rules death and shows how one will die.

Ninth House

A house of education, the rule of law, traveling a long way, and the meaning of life. The people who belong to the ninth house are usually curious and eager to learn new things. It encourages you to have an open mind and keep a watchful eye on the world around you.

Tenth House/Midheaven/Medium Sky/Medium Coeli

This house shows your image, public standing, or career. It is found at the top of the chart and tells a lot about your unique story. The individuals who belong to this house are ambitious.

Eleventh House

The house explains how you relate with your acquaintances, humanitarian projects, classes, and hopes. The development of humankind dominates this sign, both in the physical world and the ideas surrounding it.

Twelfth House

This house is about our subconscious desires, mental health, punishment, addiction, secret relationships, prison, enemies, magic, and anything hidden from others. The people born in this house are intuitive and psychic.

Interpreting the Houses of Your Birth Chart

Find the ascendant first and look for the houses corresponding to each planet in your chart. You need to understand each planet's function to begin the process.

Once you have the planet pinpointed, study what that planet represents and how that applies to the house it is in—how does the energy display itself? Since each house has a meaning, a close analysis of the chart helps you understand the connection between different houses and the birth chart. The following table highlights the meaning of each house.

House	Meaning
1ˢᵗ House	Self, vitality, appearance, and life force
2ⁿᵈ House	Resources, assets, and self-worth
3ʳᵈ House	Daily rituals, communication, siblings, and extended family
4ᵗʰ House	Home, foundations, and parents
5ᵗʰ House	Sex, creative energy, and children
6ᵗʰ House	Health and work
7ᵗʰ House	Committed partnerships
8ᵗʰ House	Mental health, death, and other people's resources
9ᵗʰ House	Travel, publishing, education, religion, philosophy, and astrology
10ᵗʰ House	Career and public activities
11ᵗʰ House	Community and good fortune
12ᵗʰ House	Loss, sorrow, and hidden life

Meaning of Astrological Houses

Astrological houses reflect a journey from your immediate self into the world. The first six houses are known as "personal houses" since they focus on self-image, daily habits, values, and ancestry. The other six houses are interpersonal since they focus on partnerships, career opportunities, travel, and the communities we build.

The First House of Self

This represents the main facets of your personality. You can look to this house for your physical representation and the main tenets of your character. Natal planets found in the first house are believed to have an effect on someone's life. For example, Mercury represents a chatterbox in the first house, while the Moon shows someone with high emotions. The first house is the first stop that marks the transition of planets, which means our goals are manifested. This gives birth to new thoughts, creativity, and the ideas needed to shape our world.

The Second House of Possessions

The house of material things, money, and worth. The house also deals with the emotions connected to these things. The house of possessions deals directly with the material, and this reflects security. While it does mainly deal with the physical, it still concerns the mental and spiritual. The house will reflect your own worth, too.

The Third House of Communication

A house of community, communing, and movement. When you utilize this house, you can forge better relationships on a small scale. Communication is vital to building friendships and is a great solution to most problems we encounter in different situations.

The Fourth House of Home and Family

We can look to our immediate surroundings with this house—dealing with our home and familial relationships within it. When we have family around us, we feel safe, secure, and loved. The house extends beyond the physical infrastructure and family bonds to include our pets and any other living beings in our home.

The Fifth House of Pleasure

A childlike house, but only in a positive way. You can find youthful energy, creativity, innocence, and romantic relationships here. If you are looking to express yourself, you can do so through this house. You can also channel this house when you want to feel more joy and happiness in your work, hobbies, or endeavors.

The Sixth House of Health

The house relates to everything to do with health and wellness. If you are looking to exercise, build muscle, or improve your body, you do so through the sixth house. Use this house when you are focusing on your work/life balance, or need to realign yourself when you have been working too hard. This house will help you to better manage your time when you are managing your schedule.

The Seventh House of Partnership

The house of change and relationships. This house includes a lot, which can affect your life in general. Things like lifelong friendships, family homes, finances, and other relationships are reflected here. This house symbolizes things like significant relationships and romantic partnerships in your life. Building strong relationships is important in our lives since it determines how we relate to other people around us. The house will also help with moving to a new job, closing any deal, or signing a contract.

The Eighth House of Sex, Death, and Transformation

The house of major transformations—death being one of them and sex being another—can change a relationship and bring new life into the world. There is also a touch of the supernatural here—another change from the physical to the spiritual—and while the house can be connected to the occult, there is nothing to fear.

You should listen to your desires and channel them appropriately, for death comes for us all. In other words, we must enjoy our short lives. However, the house reminds us to be adaptable and avoid becoming prisoners of the past. You should be ready to embrace the present and future. The planets moving through this house remind us of life's complexities and how we can deal with different situations.

The Ninth House of Philosophy

The house deals with the meaning of life, which comes from more than just philosophy—we need education and a global sense of the world, too. You must look outside who you are and the people around you to see other perspectives and ideas. People with natal planets in the ninth house are curious to know different things in life.

When this house is strong with the planets, you will find that you are more accepting of outside knowledge and may even seek it out—by study or travel. The house can encourage you to expand upon what you know, seeing things as others do not.

The Tenth House of Social Status

This house is at the peak of your birth chart, making it the end of your story—but, of course, your story does not ever end. This house is about what you want for your life—your aspirations, hopes, and dreams for the world. You can focus on this house for your ambition in your personal and professional lives.

The Eleventh House of Friendship

We need more than just work and relationships in life; we also need our friends. When you accomplish something, you must share the joy with someone close to you. The house is associated with our networks and other humanitarian pursuits. This house reminds us to remember our friends who keep us going through difficult situations.

Innovation and technology exist in this zone. If you have a strong connection to this house, you probably have large ideas that can shake the very foundations of our world.

The Twelfth House of the Unconscious

This house deals more with the metaphysical than the known world. Look to this house to help decipher your dreams, emotions, feelings, and other secrets. You may have excellent intuition within this house.

When the planets move through this house, we attract karmic people; however, they also remind us that not all relationships are designed to last. Many things happen in life and affect how we relate to others. The twelfth house is associated with Pisces energy.

Astrological Signs and Their Link to Stars of the Zodiac

Understanding the connection between houses and zodiac signs is vital since houses play crucial roles in our birth charts. Understanding the meaning of different houses helps you know the meanings of each planet and zodiac sign. There are twelve astrological houses and twelve zodiac signs, which are somehow connected. The following are the twelve astrological houses and their corresponding zodiac signs.

Aries: First House

The first house is about you and represents identity, self, appearance, and self-worth. Mars is dominant in this house and helps to drive us forward. That means that Mars also influences Aries.

Taurus: Second House

The house of personal achievement and talents. We can look to Taurus for our values and personal worth. We feel more secure and stable when we focus on this house and sign, and Venus is influential here, too. If you belong to this zodiac sign, you are surrounded by various aspects of dealing with love.

Gemini: Third House

The third house corresponds with Gemini and focuses on communication, mental processes, and intellect. This house focuses on using logic and thinking rationally to make sense. Gemini prioritizes learning in whatever form it comes. If you belong to this house, you must be keen to learn new things and explore the world around you.

Cancer: Fourth House

The fourth house is heavily influenced by the Moon but still dominated by Cancer. Look to this house for indications of family and your home. This is your foundation, your upbringing in the world, and those who have come before you. Cancer is like a string here, the Moon will guide you, and you can look to water signs, too.

Leo: Fifth House

The fifth house is mainly concerned with pleasure and is ruled by the Sun, the source of creativity. It is directly linked to Leo. This house brings a lot of pleasure in many forms—the house will guide your vacations and help with hobbies, pursuits, and children.

Virgo: Sixth House

The house of health, wealth, and daily routines. The aspects that affect your daily routine are affected by this house. Therefore, this house is related to the quality of your work in whatever you do. This house is related to Virgo, who is detail-oriented. If you belong to this zodiac sign, the chances are very high that you have an eye for detail.

Libra: Seventh House

Libra is dominant in the seventh house. This house will rule over many different types of relationships—familial, romantic, and friendships. You can also let it guide you in your business relationships.

Scorpio: Eighth House

The house of Scorpio is rooted in psychology and transformation. Look to this sign when dealing with death, change, or rebirth. This house helps with transitions in all ways—a movement from any stage of your life to another.

Sagittarius: Ninth House

The house of understanding the world on different levels—looking to the bigger questions and traveling to different places to experience different cultures. When you visit new places, you learn things other than what you are used to or comfortable with. Sagittarius rules the ninth house since it is associated with traveling. Sagittarius is also ruled by Jupiter, the planet of wisdom, luck, and travel.

Capricorn: Tenth House

The tenth house concerns status, career, social standing, and reputation. It corresponds with the goal-oriented Capricorn sign and is ruled by Saturn. It is a planet represented by the sea goat.

Aquarius: Eleventh House

The eleventh house is also known as the community house, representing fortune. It deals with hopes, groups, friends, and dreams. If you belong to this house, you will be anxious to achieve your goals. Saturn and Uranus rule the house. The eleventh house is viewed as the representation of the future. Aquarius is the zodiac sign for this house and is mainly concerned with innovation. Aquarius is also concerned about doing things better to make a difference from the popular beliefs held by many people.

Pisces: Twelfth House

The twelfth house, known as the house of secrets, deals with mysticism and seclusion. It is ruled by Pisces. People who belong to this house want to live secret lives. The house is also co-ruled by Neptune and Jupiter.

Astrological houses reflect the life journey you travel and reflect different things you encounter. This chapter explained the meanings of the twelve astrological houses and their implications on the birth chart. The chapter also highlighted the zodiac signs that rule each house and explained the importance of the relationship between the zodiac signs and each house.

Chapter 7: Align with Your Karmic Life Purpose

Finding meaning in life and being purposeful in how we treat ourselves and one another is one of the universe's greatest gifts and also one of its most puzzling mysteries. Humans' so-called search for meaning seems like a cliché, but it is truly at the heart of what drives so many of humanity's endeavors, whether individuals realize it on a practical level or not. However, what do we mean when we say, "karmic life purpose?"

You are probably wondering how it's different from the usual sayings bandied about finding our place in the world and whether our work is purposeful and positively impacts others.

This chapter devotes some time to figuring out precisely how to understand your karmic life purpose and ensure you make the most of the gift provided to you.

Our Distracted Times

We are swamped with information these days. Arguably, information that comes in a deluge is rarely useful and can have the opposite effect. Instead of feeling empowered, you feel overwhelmed and confused. Maybe the information that comes to your phone or computer without context is misinformation, rumors, and lies that do not make much sense but nonetheless leave you feeling hopeless. More than ever, we are distracted by looming wars, an ongoing pandemic, difficult economic circumstances, and empty consumerism—pretty and filtered ads that promise us the world. Yet, the products leave us feeling hollow. Our attention spans are limited and have become even more compressed in response over time because you can only retain so much information. It has made finding our purpose even harder since there's a lot of noise out there about what we should do or how to spend our time to feel productive and worthy of your community's love and respect. Sadly, that worth is sometimes tied to things like your job and salary, the house you can afford, etc. It seems that society has concluded that altruism is for suckers, and unless you join the daily hustle and grind, you are not doing meaningful work.

The messaging for millennials is arguably even more convoluted since the concept of "hustling harder" has been conflated with "doing what you love." Of course, a lot of ink has been wasted on how these disparate concepts have morphed to create much of the solipsism and silly high-mindedness of "dudebros" running Silicon Valley. Thankfully, that phase is coming to an end— partly due to the pandemic and how it has thrown these strange ideas into high relief, exposing them for the empty sloganeering they always were.

To that effect, the so-called "Great Resignation" seems to be a response colored in part by the desire to find some higher purpose, adding a deeply spiritual meaning to what we hope to accomplish on this planet before leaving it. We are still distracted by everything around us, and these are exceptionally difficult times, with good reason. However, more and more people are cutting through the sadness and despair, the capitalistic ideals of what a good person entails, and doing something that feeds their soul and helps others feel loved and safe. For centuries, humankind was largely devoted to understanding the concept of "purpose" and discovering its meaning. That philosophizing seems to have died out, and there are not as many active philosophers today whose words are consumed in the same manner as they were in the last century.

Nonetheless, despite the constant noise around us, the issue has come up again, piercing the cloud of frustration and hounding so many people. Now, people are trying to understand the karmic life's purpose and how to find theirs. Having a central purpose has helped many people live long and healthy lives for years because they feel they have something tangible to live for, a central purpose. Without it, we would feel lost and unmoored. In this deeply individualistic society, it could be heresy to say that you want to live for something other than yourself. Still, it is a risk worth taking since it will make you feel more grounded and hopeful about the world around you in the long run.

Definitions

Earlier in this book, some content was devoted to exploring the meaning of karma and how it can be applied to everyday life. As previously mentioned, karma is Sanskrit for action or deed, but spiritually it refers to the principle of cause and effect. We hear this as part of various daily phrases, explaining how karma is a... well, you know the rest. Yet that is a rather tidy and not wholly truthful definition of the word.

Karma, in principle, means focusing your intentions so they influence the world around you. Hence, if you are concerned with putting good karma out there, you should expect better karma in return—not necessarily in this life, but perhaps in the next or reincarnation. Of course, bad intentions often go hand in hand with bad deeds and will contribute to bad things coming your way. Again, that does not mean you will reap the consequences immediately—perhaps later in life or through your rebirth. For most Indian religions, karma is deeply tied to the idea of rebirth. It is in stark contrast to how the principle has been adopted in the West, wherein consequences are thought to occur here and now and not on another metaphysical plane of existence.

Now, with that refresher out of the way, it is time to pay attention to what we mean by "life's purpose" and how it is connected with the principle of karma. The first part of this chapter explained the meaning of life and humankind's search for it more generally. However, finding a spiritual purpose is slightly different from finding meaning in life—although they are somewhat linked. In truth, finding a spiritual purpose is more about becoming a better version of yourself and perhaps finding fulfilling and meaningful work, as those behind the Great Resignation will tell you—although work is one part of the equation. How we move in all areas of our lives and how we treat ourselves and others is at stake when we define this term in a spiritual sense.

It has become very easy to feel disconnected from our communities, ourselves, and our spiritual way of life. The disenchantment with organized religion has only compounded this problem, causing people to splinter into different isolated groups since they do not see themselves represented in any of the hallowed realms of mainstream religions. It can be argued that humankind's natural state is to have a deep core of spirituality at its center, and having that torn away is one of the modern tragedies of everyday life. There are many understandable reasons for this, but it is worth underscoring that finding time for personal reflection and practicing different spiritual wellness is good for the individual and the community. It allows us to harness the energy required to fight many of the injustices we see in the world. Without our spirituality, the desire to fight for what is right can be significantly weakened.

Moreover, finding and cultivating your karmic life purpose can and should be its reward. No one does it to gain anything in return. If they do, they are truly going about it in the wrong way and will be more spiritually poisoned than the rest of us who go about our days feeling numb. No one should simply exhibit signs of their spirituality but act on it privately. Seeking this purpose means you will be gracious and compassionate and strive toward self-actualization—without trying to hijack others' trauma. It also means you will work on your self-esteem and flourish in your personal relationships. For example, your circle of friends could be small; however, they include healthy relationships with proper boundaries.

Furthermore, a karmic life purpose is completely divorced from material concerns. Take your career out of the equation—unless we are talking about the specific circumstances in which your labor feels toxic or is actively harming the planet in alarming ways. In that case, it will help to eventually consider leaving your full-time job and finding something else that allows you to feel spiritually whole. Generally, material pursuits are not part of the deal here, but they can be connected. A karmic spiritual purpose is more aligned with establishing and implementing a set of values in your daily life. These guiding principles help give your life meaning and inevitably influence your decisions.

Aligning Your Karmic Life Purpose

The words "alignment" and "karma" evoke a new age, hapless approach to life that sounds too woo-woo for most people to employ or even contemplate. It brings up imagery of astrologers and palm readers—both legitimate professions but ones that do not necessarily curry favor with the majority. Also, some ideas behind living a purposeful life may seem cost-prohibitive to many people, and this imagery shrouds much of the work in the guise of elitism that is difficult to shake. Thankfully, there are different ways you can be aligned with your karmic purpose and feel part of a larger community, many of which are modest interventions that don't take up much of your time or resources.

Interestingly, millennials were always recognized as a generation with less brand loyalty than previous generations. Companies soon figured out that the way to gain their trust was to uphold an underlying cause or message behind their product. It is not to say that previous generations were not interested in finding some life purpose and ensuring that their consumer habits reflected as much—we are generally not fans of generalizations. However, it seems that the more our society relies on technology and myths around office work and productivity, the more likely younger generations will throw these concepts into question. They learned that exercising their market power was one way to feel purposeful about how they choose to live their lives. Well, there are other, more in-depth ways to align your karmic purpose, far from the pressure corporations exert on your pocketbook and conscience.

Firstly, sometimes being aligned with your karmic life purpose means allowing yourself to feel vulnerable. Brene Brown has done a great deal of research on the topic and has destigmatized the feeling of being open with others since that has often been mistaken for weakness. If you truly want something, give your heart and soul to that ideal without expectation. Furthermore, never feel detached from the spiritual work you are doing—letting yourself love and serve others while allowing them to nurture that feeling in return is key to a sense of self-worth and purpose. To become a giving person, you must be willing to receive. Trust is built on a willingness to be open, and people will not necessarily feel safe with someone determined to be closed off or unwilling to receive gratitude themselves.

It means that you should also be yourself and never be fake. Sure, keeping boundaries in place is healthy, but don't pretend to be someone you're not. Living in fear of who you are or other people's judgment will only exacerbate the feeling that you're ultimately unable to fulfill your life purpose. This may take a certain measure of courage for many of us since being honest about who you are and what you're about is not always safe or something the surrounding community may encourage. However, authenticity is part and parcel of much of the work that needs to be done here, and you will feel miserable if you're in a situation requiring you to be inauthentic or closed off to others. Living life truthfully allows you to be more open and feel more empathy for others, which, in turn, impacts how you connect with people around you.

Another way to align with your karmic purpose is always to be willing to extend a helping hand. If you can help in some way, don't hesitate. Perhaps you cannot help financially, but maybe you can help others simply by being kind, offering a shoulder to cry on, or listening to other people's concerns. Don't be judgmental or overly ideological. That seems like a tall order in our hyper-polarized world, but it does not have to be. If there is one thing you can do that can benefit others, it is to help out whenever possible. Also, always give to others without expecting anything in return.

This ties into our next point, which is to be friendly. A smile can go a long way, and spreading joy as opposed to a constant stream of negativity is always appreciated. The more good karma you put out into the universe, the more at peace you will feel. Holding onto anger and resentment without a proper outlet could make life even more difficult for you, so it helps to change your perspective slightly and be more open and loving with the universe.

Meditating daily, if only for five minutes at a time, is bound to help you feel calmer and put together, especially during difficult times. Your soul needs time to heal, and the same can be said for almost everyone these days. Meditation is arguably the only time during the day that will allow you to feel grounded and safe in your body as you work to calm yourself and feel prepared for the day ahead. If you are so inclined, try prayer since it similarly helps connect you to the universe on a deeper level. These practices are as old as time and have served a purpose for many years. Many people have benefited from meditation and the like, and it helps to remember that these are tools you can keep in your toolbox as you embark on this journey.

Given how exhausting everything feels these days, you may feel burnout and despondent. Of course, this seems to be the case with many people, and it has become part of an ongoing mental health crisis. If you're wondering how to break the cycle, one thing you can do is explore new ways of developing your creativity. Imagination is usually tapered down due to the pressures of modern life. We have to earn a living, pay off debt, and take care of our sanity in the face of an incredibly insane world. Naturally, your creativity dies amid all of this, making you feel disconnected from the people around you. Creativity isn't only about enjoying or producing arts and crafts; it's about opening yourself up to different experiences and feelings, which is key to achieving a karmic life purpose. If this sounds like you, it's okay to take some time for yourself and let your mind wander.

Alternatively, you could journal for a few minutes every day. Even if you can't afford to do so for half an hour, five minutes of simply writing down your thoughts, feelings, and observations will eventually help you unlock whatever is getting in the way. Your imagination will start to thrive again. Maybe go to a museum one day, bike to your local park, and quietly take notes of what you see. Adding a healthy dose of creativity to your life will eventually open you up to other possibilities or opportunities you may have missed entirely. This hard work will bring you into a deeper alignment with your purpose.

Think of it this way. As a kid, you were probably happy to explore new ideas and could not wait to learn something new. Stories, finger painting, watching a great movie, and playtime with friends were all activities that encouraged a sense of wonder and fondness for the universe at large. As we get older, we forget this sense of wonder, which becomes buried by the effort of simply having to live and care for ourselves in a tiresome world. Once you rediscover the things that previously brought you joy as a child, you may become more vulnerable and excited about aligning with your karmic purpose and making better sense of the world.

Reflections

There are many ways to help you feel aligned with your karmic purpose, and you can do a lot of important work to help you fulfill that endeavor. Ultimately, it is part of a quest that may take up your entire life, and your purpose may change as you evolve. So, before implementing any changes in your life, you need to ask yourself a few questions to help you achieve an enhanced spirituality. Take the following quiz to help guide you and figure out whether or not you are aligned with your karmic life purpose:

1. What is the central purpose that informs my life?
2. I want to be a good person—how should that be defined?
3. Am I connecting with the people in my life? Are there ways in which I can form stronger bonds with the people I care about?
4. Is my day job aligned with what I hope to do in life? Does it help produce impactful helpful work, or does it actively harm others, the environment, etc.?
5. Am I living in the best way possible, or are there blind spots that need to be filled?

Jot down your answers to each of these questions. Take the time to think and mull over precisely what you hope to achieve in life. Honestly, gauge where you are, and note the things you are willing to change or different approaches you can implement. Practicing empathy, compassion, and willingness to be vulnerable is not easy and can take a long time to achieve. Putting pen to paper and being more mindful of yourself and the world around you is an important step in the right direction.

Chapter 8: Understanding and Integrating Karmic Lessons

Karmic cycles are patterns of feelings, emotions, situations, and realizations that you experience repetitively throughout your life. They present themselves as opportunities to unlock a higher level of consciousness or wisdom and ultimately break negative cycles in your life. Karmic lessons will keep repeating themselves until you have finally understood and mastered the lesson at hand so that you avoid the same pitfalls time and time again.

Practitioners of New Age or Indian spirituality, yoga, and astrology are at least familiar with the term Karmic lessons (or cycles). However, this concept may seem rather foreign for those new to the world of spirituality and healing practice. Regardless of your level of expertise, grasping a deeper understanding of the concepts of karma and karmic lessons is necessary if you want to embark on your healing journey.

As you may have guessed, the idea of karmic lessons and cycles initially sprouts from the concept of karma. As you may recall from Chapter One, karma, as a concept, is the essence of numerous Indian religions like Buddhism, Hinduism, Sikhism, and Jainism. When mentioned in a spiritual context, the word typically means something greater than its literal meaning. Karma is a large part of our lives. It focuses on our actions and intentions. Even if we think of an act and do not carry it out, karma still works through that, so it is important to think good thoughts as well as do good deeds.

Thinking positive thoughts can bring about positive outcomes. On the other hand, bad actions and intentions create bad karma, resulting in negative outcomes. Those with positive intentions, who take actions with unintentionally negative outcomes, can create good karma for themselves. In other words, "What goes around, comes around."

Reincarnation and Karmic Cycles

You are probably familiar with the concept of reincarnation in Eastern religions. According to theology, we have all lived several lifetimes, each granting us a chance to grow and work on ourselves for the better. Unfortunately, growth cannot happen overnight. It takes time, effort, and change to become the best versions of ourselves. We must emerge successfully from a series of spiritual, ethical, and moral challenges, otherwise known as karmic cycles.

The experiences, events, and situations we could not deal with correctly during our previous lifetimes take the shape of karmic lessons. We must learn our intended lessons, whether we've failed to put energies into their best use, overcome certain obstacles, made the wrong choices, or discarded potentially life-changing opportunities. Until we do so, these learning opportunities will keep presenting themselves. Once we master the lessons, our life experiences become easier to manage, and we are generally much happier and more joyful. Let us say that you failed to manage a moral challenge in a past lifetime, where societal pressures, fear, or even a lack of knowledge caused you to act contradictory to your morals. A karmic cycle will present similar challenges to you in your current lifetime. These dilemmas appear in your life's professional, familial, romantic, or societal aspects.

In this chapter, you will learn more about karmic lessons and cycles and what you can learn from them. Here, you will come across the signs accompanying karmic lessons to help you identify whether you're experiencing one. Finally, you will learn how to integrate these lessons into your life.

What Can I Learn from a Karmic Cycle?

You may wonder how learning from something you do not remember doing will benefit you. What good will it do if you're forced to learn from situations that a previous reincarnation of yourself mishandled or issues left unresolved for lifetimes?

Well, karmic cycles are typically intended to teach you three main lessons: Staying in touch with your morals and values, staying true to yourself, and trusting the journey. Karmic lessons aim to teach you your role in certain life situations. The main point is to learn to take full responsibility for your actions, behaviors, thoughts, and emotions.

Once you have mastered a karmic lesson, you will realize you're the only person who can walk your unique path in life. No one will be coming in to push you, motivate you, or help you find happiness. It is up to you to use your intuition, harness your strength, work on self-development, and seek happiness. You're meant to be independent and transparent. Living your truth is the only way to break the cycle and take on the challenge. These challenges are not easy to emerge triumphantly. If they were, you would not still be facing them in this lifetime. Instead of resenting or denying the need to learn, you must accept that you are destined to learn and grow from these obstacles. Humbling yourself and embracing those karmic cycles is the key to approaching these lessons with honor. You must garner your inner strength and believe in your ability to grow to succeed.

Signs You're Experiencing a Karmic Lesson

Every step we take in life, whether positive or negative, has an outcome and leads to a consequence. So, there is always a lesson to be learned. Good deeds come with immediate positive consequences that urge us to do more of this good action. On the other hand, negative outcomes are often harder to learn, particularly because very few people realize they are experiencing a karmic lesson. Fortunately, some signs are there to help you determine whether there's a life lesson to be learned.

Things Feel Oddly Familiar

The easiest way to determine whether you are experiencing a karmic lesson is to look for patterns. If you're experiencing a karmic cycle, you will probably feel like your life events revolve around the same themes. Take a moment to think about the problems you face in different aspects of your life, whether in your career, relationship, or family. Do you have stagnant energy when these problems arise?

Perhaps your partner reminds you of a toxic parent, or you constantly find yourself stuck in detrimental work environments. Maybe your destructive cycle creates the same unhealthy environment you grew up in. Do you find yourself chugging on alcohol every night as your father did?

Detrimental cycles and patterns are not purely spiritual. According to psychology, generational and childhood traumas and personal attachment styles can lead to unhelpful behavioral loops. These loops are what we refer to as karmic cycles in spirituality. We must identify the patterns, learn their triggers, and trace them back to a cause to break the cycle.

You Lack Control

How often do you feel like you have no control over your life or at least some aspects of it? You try your best to go down a certain path or make what you think is the right choice. However, going according to plan becomes nearly impossible, and you have to go the other way. Karmic lessons leave you with no choices. They force you to go in a certain direction, even if it is the opposite of what you want, because they want you to see the full picture. In most cases, a karmic lesson will force you to see something you're unaware of.

Things do not always work out. However, if you notice this becoming a pattern, you need to take a step back and ask yourself where you went wrong because this is karma in action.

You're Stuck in a Karmic Relationship

When a karmic lesson is in the works, you will encounter a person you believe you cannot live without. At first, everything will feel like a dream. You'll feel you are destined to be together. However, your hopes and dreams about the relationship started falling apart shortly after. At one point, saving the relationship becomes impossible, no matter how hard you try to patch things up. You'll still hope and try to work things out even then because you cannot help but think your life will be over once that person leaves. Karma will test you by continuously sending this person into your life until you have finally learned your lesson.

You Always Attract Similar People

Whether it's a friend or a romantic partner, think about the people you attract into your life. Do all partners share similar traits? Perhaps your current significant other shares your father's controlling tendencies or your mother's manipulative ways. Psychology reveals that we are naturally drawn toward people, situations, and even emotions that make us feel comfortable, even when they always lead us to the same traumatic cycle. We are attracted to the familiar even when it hurts.

If you grew up in an environment where anger issues were a major concern, the feeling you get, no matter how bad, is incredibly familiar when you see your partner getting angry. So, you tolerate it even when it brings you pain. If you grew up with parents who didn't fulfill your emotional needs, you might feel the most comfortable in relationships lacking emotional intimacy, those that make you feel lonely.

You're Always Facing Your Fears

Have you noticed that most situations you find yourself in bring out at least a couple of your worst fears? Do these events make you wonder whether you'll actually make it out alive? You can't seem to shut down your thoughts to the point where you have to experience multiple sleepless nights. No solution seems viable enough to get you out of this mess. Unless you pinpoint the lesson at hand and master it, you cannot find a solution.

Let us take financial insecurity as an example. Suppose your mind is often preoccupied with monetary problems. In that case, you could end up settling for jobs that bring you no happiness or emotional fulfillment for years just to guarantee stability and financial security. At the same time, you can't shake away visions of your dream job in your mind.

If you're continuously facing problems in your current job or even lose it, this is a karmic opportunity presenting itself. You have two choices: Search for other jobs that promise financial security but lack emotional fulfillment, or take a leap of faith and do what you've always wanted to do. Unless you make the latter choice and face your fears, you will remain stuck in the same karmic cycle. As mentioned above, karmic cycles teach you to garner the strength and courage to be true to yourself. You must always think of these events as opportunities to re-evaluate your choices, current life situation, and desires.

It Feels Your Loved Ones Are Turning against You

If you're still persistent in keeping the lesson unlearned, karma will take drastic measures to ensure you break your cycle. You must know it's time to take the reins and change things around when you feel those closest to you are turning against you. Whether your partner acts impulsively or your best friend acts irrationally, you feel compelled to act unlike yourself. Going against your true nature and doing things you would not normally do indicates a lesson to be learned.

Your Darkest Side Seems to Be Making Its Way Out

We are not typically fully aware of how we react in certain situations unless we experience them. Most of the time, we aren't aware of the extent or extremity of our reactions. Unfortunately, karmic lessons have a way of pushing us to the edge. They keep pressuring us until we lash out, causing the most undesirable, spiteful, and unfavorable traits to surface. It can be a side of you that you never even knew existed.

Karmic Lessons Are a Gateway to Healing

A karmic cycle makes its way into your life to help you attain a higher level of consciousness—ultimately, one that accompanies a greater level of moral and ethical judgment in your current lifetime. Believe it or not, karmic lessons are primarily meant to help you heal. They can be very painful to endure. However, once you overcome them, you'll emerge much stronger, wiser, and more independent. These lessons are meant to help you unlock your full potential and become a better version of yourself. You take major steps toward achieving wholeness once you decide to work on the mental, spiritual, and emotional aspects of your being. With this effort, you'll self-actualize and heal yourself on a much deeper level.

This journey is not easy to tackle on your own. So, we recommend reaching out to a mental health professional (one who respects your spiritual beliefs, of course) to point you in the right direction. A mental health professional can help you point out troublesome patterns more easily. They also help you determine where they come from, what triggers them, and why it's so hard for you to break these cycles. It's important to understand that doing this therapy can be distressing. It's also very hard to get out of your comfort zone and make different choices. Having a professional by your side will provide much-needed support when things get rough. You should also consider holistic therapy since it focuses on optimizing your physical, emotional, spiritual, and mental health.

Things to Keep in Mind

Whether you choose to walk this path on your own or seek help, you must always focus on your relationship with yourself throughout this process. Try your best to practice self-compassion and avoid being overly critical of yourself. Make it your priority to unleash your authentic self and align with your values. Making it to the other side of a karmic lesson is very challenging. Continuously developing the connection with your authentic, most genuine self will give you strength. However, it can increase your chances of breaking these detrimental cycles.

You can change your life just by bringing a karmic cycle to an end. All you need are the right actions, intentions, support, and, most importantly, perspective. Hopefully, you will notice a gradual positive shift in your life circumstances over time. It helps to keep in mind that the essence of karmic lessons extends beyond lifetimes. Once you break free from the loops holding you back, working toward personal growth and development becomes a lot easier. You'll notice your career, lifestyle, and romantic and social relationships elevating in the process.

It is not enough to merely acknowledge that you are experiencing a karmic cycle you need to break. It's no more than one step toward creating change, and learning your lesson is half the equation. You must integrate what you learned into your life to heal fully.

Breaking a Karmic Cycle

To break a karmic cycle, you should be able to recognize it first. Take a moment to reflect on the problematic areas of your life and note any signs mentioned above. Analyze your personal relationships and understand why you feel stuck in this cycle. It will help you determine what lessons you need to learn.

Practicing self-compassion and acceptance is also vital when breaking a karmic cycle. One of the most important things a karmic lesson will teach you is that you must always prioritize your needs in any relationship or situation. Often, we fail to voice our wants and concerns, fearing we may hurt others. Unfortunately, this causes us to push our values, beliefs, and convictions aside.

You can only overcome a karmic lesson by trusting your intuition. Only then will you precisely know what you expect and deserve in any relationship. Your intuition is never wrong, so trust it to guide you to the right path. Breaking a karmic cycle can be broken down into the following five steps.

How to Integrate Your Karmic Lesson

1. Get in Touch with Your Values

Problems will always happen when you are not yourself or not aligning with your values. It is easier to push everything we stand for aside just so we can please the community, make friends, or avoid unnecessary arguments. However, you must take full responsibility for your authentic self, actions, beliefs, behaviors, and thoughts to unlock your full potential.

2. Be Self-Compassionate

We are our worst enemies. Nothing holds us back more than that loud, demanding, and critical voice inside our minds. How do you expect to move forward or work toward personal growth and development when you constantly doubt your abilities? Practicing self-compassion and working toward self-love helps you integrate your karmic lessons. When you're self-compassionate, you learn to trust yourself, your faith increases, and so does your strength. Without self-compassion, you will continue to settle for less.

3. Live for No One Else but Yourself

We all fall into the trap of caring about what others think of us before we take any steps forward. We worry about letting others down or disappointing them even when we are doing what is best for us. We let others determine our path and listen to the advice of others because we doubt our choices. Sometimes, you need to take a step back and realize you're the only person who can decide what's best on your journey. You need to start searching for your own happiness.

4. Lean into Your Intuition and Work on Your Independence

Learning to listen to your intuition and maintaining your independence is the only way you'll fall in tune with your truth. You cannot be your true self if you do not trust yourself or depend on others for direction.

5. Trust the Journey

As explained above, you must embrace that you are destined to learn your karmic lesson. The process is not easy. However, you should not stress because everything unfolds the way it should.

Breaking a karmic cycle requires you to make many significant and uncomfortable changes in your life. Taking these drastic measures isn't easy to tolerate, especially when you may feel compelled to avoid your problems and go back to your old ways. However, it helps to remember the pain that comes with avoiding emotional aspects. Experiencing these karmic cycles over and over is much worse than facing your fears and putting an end to the lesson once and for all.

Chapter 9: Astrological Predictions

A common misconception is that astrology is a new age concept with no bearing in reality or that a mystic practice is more akin to fortune-telling than anything else. This is not a half-truth but rather a flat-out lie obfuscating that true astrology is based on several scientific disciplines and mystical principles. The practice is a complicated exploration of the solar system and how our personalities and life trajectories are tied to the universe. Of course, plenty of bad astrologers out there have contributed to the study's bad name. People writing horoscopes in the vast majority of newspapers and magazines are the same ones who write dodgy messages for fortune cookies from their cramped at-home offices. However, professional astrologers are a different breed, and many are good at what they do and take their work very seriously. Part of that work is using astrology to determine predictions helpful to their clients. Some of the tools they use are complicated and particularly involved, but it is possible to make astrological predictions on your own, provided you have a few basic concepts nailed down. This chapter will help make this work feel more accessible and provide you with a few vital tools that will make it much easier to get the benefits of astrological predictions yourself.

How Astrological Predictions Work

In the simplest terms, astrology is the study of the movements and positions of celestial bodies—the stars and planets—and how they are interpreted in their capacity to influence human life and the natural world. The practice of astrology holds that many answers people look for can be found by simply looking up and making notes of the sky. The word prediction means forecasting a particular event or occurrence. In this sense, it is more about checking something like the weather forecast instead of looking into a crystal ball and telling the future. A prediction is just that—a forecast and nothing more. People conflate what an astrological prediction entails, but the reality is something far more grounded than what appears in mainstream books or television shows. An astrological prediction is a way of finding your way through the fog, and if it suddenly rains, well, at least you are prepared.

So, an astrological prediction definitely does not provide you with knowledge of the future. Rather, it presents a series of guideposts to help you better understand certain situations and how best to react or decide according to the context. For example, a popular astrological prediction is a horoscope. Astrologers typically write these—well, the good ones—and they are presented according to the sun signs. It's nothing more complicated than that. Most legit horoscopes are presented monthly rather than weekly and give you vague ideas on how certain events will make you feel.

Let us say you're an Aquarius. A sample horoscope may read something like this:

These days you find yourself distracted by a wide array of wonderfully compelling people, places, and concepts. They provide a tangible way of distancing yourself from your emotional needs, which can be convenient. Since you're not the type that enjoys being terribly introspective, you could find yourself using most of your energies to connect with others rather than focus on your interior life. That is all well and good, but remember, you should be as generous and non-judgmental of yourself as you are of others. Doing some thinking and taking care of your needs doesn't mean you're selfish. Work to shift your perspective, and note that you are just as worthy of respect and intellectual curiosity as everyone else.

This kind of horoscope writing may seem familiar to you. Much advice is in the realm of the conceptual, and precious little has anything to do with something concrete happening to you at the moment. However, if you take the horoscope for what it's worth, you will realize that much of this seemingly general advice is probably something you could listen to at the moment. That is the thing: Astrological predictions can take the form of advice and offer guidance on how to deal with things you are struggling with. An astrological prediction, be it a horoscope or anything else, is not like something out of a playbook by Nostradamus, e.g., "The universe will end in the year 2000." Of course, Nostradamus was a talented astrologer; however, his predictions have sometimes been taken out of context or misinterpreted by the powers that be to denote other things he probably did not intend to bring into the popular conversation. The point is that a prediction is rarely—if ever—a way to tell you what will happen tomorrow, next week, or the following year. They are bits of information based on your sun sign and the planetary movements in the sky, offering you spiritual guidance to help better make sense of where your life is at.

How to Make Astrological Predictions

Providing a forecast of the future is no easy feat, and it is usually based on very precise tools astrologers use to decipher what their clients should expect in the coming months. Several techniques are used to make an astrological prediction, some of which are based on transits, progressions, and returns.

Before we get into these techniques in-depth, it helps to uncover the tools typically used in drafting astrological predictions in the first place. For one, you will need an ephemeris. In the practice of astronomy and understanding of celestial navigation, an ephemeris is a book that contains tables providing you with the trajectory of naturally occurring astronomical objects, and even artificial satellites in the sky, over a particular period. Some books cover enough information to last a few years; however, most are devoted to making things tangible for hundreds of years at a time. An ephemeris is required for spacecraft making their way to a mission in outer space, but astrologers also use it to help navigate the complex realities of the stars and planets as they relate to sun and moon signs. They are a key part of any serious astrologer's toolkit in understanding how to make an astrological prediction for themselves or others.

The next thing you need, arguably the most important tool in your arsenal, is a birth chart. A natal or birth chart shows the placement of the planets when you were born. That placement helps you to understand who you are and the journey you are on. You will need your date of birth, the location, and the exact time you were born to create a birth chart. If you are unsure of the time, choose an estimate or start at twelve noon. Then, draw the planets and the houses. If this seems too complex, use an online free birth chart template, which will have the correct information for you.

The birth chart will ultimately look like a twelve-slice pie. Each slice is referred to as a house. Each house is associated with a sign of the zodiac. And each zodiac influences your life. The sections in the middle are called aspects and depict how natal planets in your chart communicate with one another. For example, you may have a Taurus sun sign, but your moon sign is Pisces, and your rising sign is Leo. Each informs different parts of your personality and provides important signposts for how different aspects of your life will play out. Each aspect will have a different shape, line, and color and come together at various intersecting points. Depending on the thickness of the line, you can understand how strong a particular connection will be and what to infer from that based on other pieces of information you have on hand.

To read a birth chart, you need to look at three things in unison: Each planet and its concurrent sun sign, the house the planet resides in, and the connections each planet makes with other planets. This information will reveal intricate details about who you are, your fears, strengths, family, childhood, etc.

This now brings us to the techniques mentioned earlier and how they make astrological predictions. Transits are perhaps the easiest to understand of the three complex techniques. If you want to predict what will happen to someone on a given day, all you do is compare the positions of the planets in the sky to their positions in their birth chart. So, the position of the planets moving in the sky is called transiting planets. If your birth chart reads that Pluto is at twenty degrees of Aquarius and transiting Venus, it means that today is a Pluto-Venus day for you, which could be a good time to relax at home and do some gardening, cooking, etc.

Progressions are a bit trickier; however, they function slightly similarly. An astrologer uses different progressions, but the most common is a day for a year progression, sometimes referred to as a secondary progression. This progression is calculated by adding one day to the date of birth for each year of the person's life. This technique allows you to look to the future, maybe ten years from now, and read what the secondary chart predicts will happen at that time. Perhaps there will be a major milestone or the unfurling of a romantic relationship.

Other progressions astrologers use could be the day for a month or tertiary progression. This progress chart adds to the date of birth for each month of life. There is also the solar arc direction, which is not used as often given its complexity, but astrologers also refer to it for guidance. It entails looking at the planets, how they move or rotate within the solar system, and how that pertains to the information on a birth chart.

The last popular technique in astrological prediction is the return. This marks when a transiting planet returns to its position at birth. So, if your sun position is twelve degrees and fifteen minutes of Cancer, the Sun will return to the same position every year around your birthday. Based on this information, a chart is created and used to foretell various issues you need to be mindful of annually. Likewise, the Moon should return to the same position at birth every month, and a chart created for this purpose is referred to as a lunar return chart. This technique pays homage to how certain elements of our life trajectory are circular and part and parcel of the same package, time and again.

Decoding Planetary Transits

For this section and easier digestion, let us briefly go back to the easier concept—astrological transits, and how they help inform your birth chart. The following is a sample of how it could look:

Planets: Venus, Pluto, Jupiter

Natal: 7 - 2

Rules: 9 - 3,8

Moon: 56 - 24

Sun: 4 - 3,1

Of course, this is just the beginning of the work, and you will come across different iterations you need to jot down as you move to the chart. Again, most charts are fairly complicated, so compare various online resources with the templates clearly set out for you. You need to enter some basic biographical data about yourself, and then you can move forward based on what has already been provided. One helpful thing about inputting this data online is that you can also run the birth and transit chart and search for a specific future date to determine what you may encounter at that point in time. An ephemeris is also helpful since it provides a more detailed account of the daily planetary movements and when planets are leaving a specific transit. In layperson's terms, when the planetary return will put the planet's position in the same position as it was at your birth.

This is all fairly complicated, and looking at the wheel of your birth chart can be overwhelming. However, if you take the time to look closely at what each piece of information is telling you, you will eventually know how to crack the codes the universe sets out for each of us at our birth. Astrology is a complex science, and you must also have a strong grasp of astronomy and some of the more mystical branches of religion and psychic studies to have a holistic view of what a chart is telling you. Generally, you can learn a great deal by making a few simple interventions and using a birth chart to your advantage. Luckily, many online resources are making more of these underpinnings accessible and digestible beyond the book in your hands.

Furthermore, much of this work is about practicing. Once you have studied the planets and houses and understood each sign's characteristics, you can pull out an ephemeris and sketch different ideas to help you better navigate how the solar system speaks to your experiences and personality traits. The birth chart is the carrier of so many secrets, and in that sense, you can decode different aspects of your life and figure out astrological predictions that make the most sense to you.

People have turned to astrology to predict the future for a millennium. Following celestial patterns and movements in the sky is a precise technique that requires the practitioner to exhibit great compassion and responsibility. Whether you make predictions for yourself or others, you need a detail-oriented approach to the art form. Sometimes, our obsession with predictions reveals more about our anxieties than anything else, and it is important to acknowledge that dissonance as you make astrological predictions.

If you think that ethical concerns around astrological predictions are overblown, consider this: For a long while, rulers of empires have historically relied upon astrologers as a way of maintaining their power. If the astrologer communicated unfavorable information, many were imprisoned or even killed. So, the ability to bring a certain level of precision and care into the practice of astrology is important and often referred to as a necessity.

Furthermore, people think that making astrological predictions will tell you what will happen in the future and possibly even provide tips on avoiding horrific events. Well, astrology does not result in pat resolutions. In reality, you would be better off thinking about astrology as making forecasts rather than predictions. The main difference is that astrology allows for a more thematic and interpretive guide to reading what might happen in the future. In this sense, horoscopes are a good example since they provide an idea of what could happen to you according to your sun sign, but they will not say something as straightforward as, "Someone will propose to you on May twenty-first."

It's worth remembering that regardless of how precise the work behind astrology is, the astrological prediction will not help you predict a future event or anything concrete. Rather, it provides a general idea of when to expect a major milestone and guidance on handling it depending on your personality traits and history. You would be setting expectations for yourself and others about dealing with different issues and plan to move forward from there. Always remember that the concept of free will is at play, and merely because something happens to you doesn't mean that you need to go through with it or not work to alter the lead-up to that event. The decision is ultimately yours, and you can make the right one depending on the information.

Chapter 10: Reincarnation — The Law of Karmic Return

Reading this book, you are likely to have already encountered the idea of reincarnation and the law of karmic return. However, while other chapters touched on this concept momentarily, you should be know much more concerning these two ideas.

If you're struggling with understanding how karma and reincarnation are tied together and what the law of karmic return means, do not worry—you're in the right place. This chapter will cover everything you need to know and give you a chance to re-test how good your karma is to see how you have changed by reading and following this book.

Understanding Reincarnation and the Law of Karmic Return

Before you understand how karma and reincarnation are tied together, you will first need to understand what these ideas mean beyond the definition of the two terms.

According to the Cambridge English Dictionary, reincarnation means the belief that the soul or spirit of a dead person can return to life, not in their body, but in another body, following their death.

In Hinduism and other Indian religious traditions, reincarnation also has a spiritual element. The first reference to reincarnation is found in the Upanishads, Hindu texts that predate Buddhism and Jainism. While the idea of reincarnation differs between Hindu traditions, Hinduism generally holds that the body and the soul are different. While the physical body dies, the soul does not. The soul is indestructible.

Additionally, it should be noted that the Hindu idea of the soul is slightly different from the soul found in Western philosophies. In Western philosophies, the soul includes a person's mental abilities, including feelings, memories, thinking, etc. In Hinduism, these elements are part of a person's material self or body. Rather, the soul is the innermost self, a person's inner essence that remains unaffected by your personality and ego.

Jainism and Buddhism are similar in their ideas of the soul to Hinduism. However, in Buddhism, the soul (or atman) is not permanent, unlike in Hinduism. While there is rebirth, no permanent atman ties your lives together. Rather, there is impermanence, and everything that constitutes a being dissolves at death, after which they are reborn. In Jainism, the soul (or jiva) begins its journey in a primordial state, and as it goes through the cycles of birth and rebirth, it evolves with each rebirth.

With Hinduism, we do not think about a split afterlife. Instead, your karma affects your afterlife. You can end up in heaven if you have done good things, in hell if you have done bad, or back on Earth to grow further on your journey. As you do more good, you will become a better and better human. Furthermore, the circumstances of your future lives also depend on your karma.

However, this rebirth is not permanent—even the gods and demons die and are reborn depending on their karma. This cycle of birth, death, and rebirth continues until a person achieves the spiritual knowledge and good karma needed to attain moksha, a state of utter bliss and an escape from the reincarnation cycles.

Buddhism's tradition of rebirth is similar to Hindu traditions in that your karma affects your rebirth, and the cycle of birth, death, and rebirth is endless. In Buddhism, it is only through achieving nirvana that one can be liberated from this cycle.

In Jainism, karma holds even greater importance than in Hinduism and Buddhism. It's intricately connected to Jain philosophies, and like Buddhism and Hinduism, your karma influences your current and future lives. Additionally, some souls are thought to exist in a state of abhavya, or incapability—these souls are incapable of ever achieving moksha or liberation. A soul enters the state of abhavya after it intentionally performs an act of great evil.

Jains hold that there are four states of existence or birth categories. A person can be reborn; asdevas or demigods, manusya orhumans; tiryanca oranimals, plants and microorganisms; and naraki, which means beings of hell.

These beings live in a vertically tiered universe—the demigods at the top and beings of hell at the bottom. The better your karma, the higher on the tiers you will be reborn, and the better your circumstances will be when you are reborn. The Jain text Bhagvati sutra specifies what actions lead to what form of rebirth—violence, the killing of creatures, and eating of animals and fish lead to rebirth as a being of hell while telling lies and engaging in deception and fraud results in rebirth in the world of animals and plants. Being kind and humble results in rebirth as a human, and being austere and living a life of devotion and faithfulness to Jain tenets leads to rebirth as a demigod.

As with Hinduism and Buddhism, it's possible to be liberated from the cycle of birth and rebirth by letting go of attachments and following the fourteen stages on the path to liberation (known as Gunasthana). Some versions of Jainism hold that a soul must undergo 8,400,000 birth situations before attaining moksha. However, because we do not know where our soul is currently, we should always strive to follow the path of Gunasthana.

Sikhism's concept of karma and rebirth is relatively different from those held by the other major Indian religions. Like the other three religions, Sikhism also believes in a cycle of birth, death, and rebirth. Similarly, your karma from one life affects your circumstances in your future lives. However, your karma only influences your future lives. It's possible to attain liberation from the cycle of birth and rebirth through devotion to a god rather than a specific path to be free of attachments and gain good karma. Sikhism encourages devotion to a god to obtain mukti or liberation.

The law of karmic return has remained relatively similar across the major Indian religions. As mentioned above, the concept of reincarnation holds that the karma of your past and current lives will impact your future lives, but only at the influencing level of future lives, as in Sikhism, or determining the form of your rebirth and possibly attaining liberation from the cycle of birth and rebirth, as in Hinduism. However, through all four major Indian religions, your karma plays a major role in your future life.

Therefore, these religions hold that performing actions that provide you with good karma is essential. The better your karma, the better your future lives will be—conversely, the worse your karma, the worse off you will be in the future, in this life, or a life in the far-off future. Every action you take will impact you, even if that impact is not immediate.

The law of karmic return is not a system of punishment and reward; rather, it is simply a law underlining the consequences of a person's actions. For example, in Jainism, a god does not influence your destiny. Instead, all your life circumstances result from your karma. This is also known as the law of cause and effect or the law of action and reaction. It essentially means that everything you put into the world, you receive back in the future, both good and bad.

How Karma Affects Your Current Life

Given the idea of reincarnation, it is easy to believe that the karma you earn in your present life will not impact your future lives. However, there are two considerations to keep in mind:

- Not all karma affects future lives—you may feel the effect of some part of your earned karma in this life.
- The karma from your past lives could be affecting your current life. So, if you consider the good and bad of your current life, keep in mind that your actions similarly affect a future reincarnation of yourself.

Understanding how karma affects your current life offers you the chance to take action to mitigate these effects or act in a way to gain "positive" karma. Here are five ways your karma is affecting your current life:

1. Since karma has no expiration date, there is a good chance that some or all of your current life events result from your soul's actions in a past life (or lives). Think of it like baggage you carry through a long trip—or, in terms of your soul, a trip through multiple reincarnations. Your bag gets heavier or lighter as you add to (take actions resulting in earning karma, negatively and positively) and subtract from it (experience the effects of past karma). You ideally want to go through life with as light a karmic load as possible—requiring you to go through and confront your past karma. This is what karmic astrology offers.

2. No person in your life is there by coincidence. Karma means the role of everyone in your life is due to your past actions. Each is meant to teach you a specific lesson. In particular, karmic relationships will play out as planned regardless of your actions. Therefore, understanding your karma and its effect (if any) on your relationships enables you to move through this plan and start new relationships on your own terms.

3. The law of karmic return means that your actions affect your current life circumstances. However, it's essential to keep in mind that these circumstances are not only affected by your negative karma but also your positive karma. So, it's crucial to live an authentic, truthful life, enabling you to move past negative karma from a past life and start your future lives with positive karma.

4. The effect of karma often causes a reversal of roles in rebirth. For example, your parent may have been your child in a former life, while a close friend may have been someone you disliked. Even if you had a relationship with the people you know today in your respective past lives, these relationships and their impact on you might have been very different. You should approach your current relationships with the perspective that your souls are connected through lifetimes, including in future lives. Act according to how you want your future relationships with them to unfold.

5. As you have probably guessed from the above ways karma affects your current life, karma repeats through lifetimes. You know the same people and share similar relationships as you move through life. It raises several questions. Why do similar events happen through lifetimes? What should you do to break this pattern of repetition and similarity? The repetition of karma teaches you to take different actions to achieve different results. You will need to undergo true introspection and evaluate your strengths and weaknesses to determine what you can change. Change from the inside will also lead to external change, allowing you to modify and alter karma patterns. This is where karmic astrology comes in, and this modification allows you (and future you) to live your life (or lives) your way without the burden of your past lives weighing you down.

Things You Can Do to Attract Good Karma

Are you wondering how you can attract good karma? There are numerous positive actions you can take, including:

- Practice kindness and compassion for yourself and others.
- Forgive yourself and others.
- Complement others.
- Give people good recommendations.
- Volunteer.
- Help someone find a job.
- Thank others for their help.
- Donate something valuable to a good cause (monetary or another value like your time).
- Teach someone something. It does not have to mean book learning; it could be something as simple as teaching a friend to brew a fresh cup of tea.
- Listen to others when they talk to you.
- Show up for other people.
- Reflect and introspect on your actions.

Attracting good karma essentially requires you to be kind and compassionate to others. Any actions you take that put these concepts into action will attract good karma. At the same time, avoid harming others, including non-human creatures. Harm to others attracts negative karma, and consciously avoiding it reduces your negative karma significantly, especially since the intention is a part of what earns you negative karma.

How Good Is Your Karma?

You might have taken the "How Good Is Your Karma?" quiz in the first chapter. However, now that you know more about karmic astrology and karma in general, you have likely taken steps to ensure you attract positive karma and curtail negative karma.

It would be advisable to retake the quiz as it will allow you to understand better where you currently stand and what actions you still need to take to earn further positive karma.

Answer each question truthfully and tally your results based on the instructions at the end of the quiz.

1. You find a wallet abandoned on the train. You decide to:

a) Find the owner.

b) Leave it where it is—someone will come and get it soon.

c) Take out some money and return the wallet.

d) Keep it for yourself.

2. Do you talk to homeless people?

a) I would if I needed to

b) Perhaps a "hi" as I walk past.

c) I'd feel a bit nervous doing so.

d) Never

3. You do someone a favor. Do you:

a) Let it stay a secret—you're doing it for them, not for the acknowledgment.

b) Let them know but downplay your efforts—you'd like a little acknowledgment but aren't interested in being the center of attention.

c) Ensure you let the person you helped know—after all, you did it, so they would be aware that you liked them.

d) Make sure the person you helped knows—you want to ensure they know to pay you back in the future.

4. You encounter a lost and confused tourist on the street. You:

a) Walk with them to their destination.

b) Offer to help with directions.

c) Ignore them and power walk past.

d) Point and laugh at their predicament with your friends.

5. Do you return books from the library on time?

a) I return them early more often than not.

b) I generally return them on time, but I have been late on occasion.

c) I try returning them on time, but it's hard, and I'm generally late.

d) I can't remember the last time I returned a library book after checking it out.

6. Do you volunteer?

a) As much as I can.

b) Occasionally, but I don't have much time to spare.

c) I've considered it but have decided against it.

d) Never—I have a limited time and need to focus on making money.

7. Do you recycle?

a) Always.

b) As much as possible, though I do slack off occasionally.

c) When it's convenient.

d) Never.

8. Your best friend is going through a significant breakup. Do you:

a) Hang out with them, be there for them, and listen to them for as long as possible.

b) Spend some time with them and take them out for a meal or two.

c) Take them out a couple of times.

d) Offer to split a round of drinks.

9. Would you agree to work at a company whose mission you morally disagreed with in return for a significant salary?

a) No.

b) I'd consider it, but I'd need a lot more information.

c) I'd donate some of my paychecks, but yes.

d) Yes.

10. Do you think people should judge others based on a single action?

a) No.

b) Depends on the action in question.

c) I think judging others on their actions is justified.

d) Yes—an illegal act should always be given the full book, regardless of personal situations

When you have finished the quiz, check your answers and list how many times you got each letter—so, how many a's, etc. The letter you get the most frequently is what you should concentrate on.

The earlier your letter, the better your karma. So, if you got more a's than other letters, you have the best possible karma. If you have more d's, you need to do some work.

Moreover, it's essential to keep in mind that even if you got all a's, you still have work to do. Do not slack off on your kindness and compassion, and work to keep attracting positive karma to lighten your existing karmic load and start your next life as much on the positive side of the column as possible.

Conclusion

Like any language, the language of karmic astrology has its own rules and style, and it takes some practice to get the hang of it. Moreover, it also includes many technical concepts like the different ideas we covered. To make the most of this knowledge, you must understand it at a deeper level and practice it frequently to see real-life results. Karmic astrology is not an answer for the rest of your life; it is a practice you can use daily to make better sense of life. By understanding how karmic astrology works out for the smaller events in your life, you can understand how reading will translate to bigger events.

Unlike palmistry and other pseudosciences, karmic astrology does not merely rely on guesswork. Throughout this book, you will have noticed that it requires a lot of highly accurate information for the reading to be precise. Even a difference in a day in the birth chart can completely change the readings. Slightly altering the time of an event can have dramatically different results. Since there are so many variables at work, it's imperative to have the most accurate information to do good readings.

You need to factor in exceptions whenever you interpret karmic astrology for yourself or someone else. There are always those Sagittarius individuals who are terrible at saving money and are extremely hyper. Even when you have done everything perfectly, you will find your results are not translating correctly. This may just be an exceptional case; it doesn't have to be a fault on your end.

While we have covered a lot of information in this book, it's always helpful to supplement your learning through other sources. There is plenty of material available on karmic astrology, and you can learn a great deal of detail on any subject of your choice. When consulting other sources, keep in mind that different practitioners have different methods of interpreting. While there is no hard and fast rule about how something can be defined, the information in this book gives you a clear direction. If you find another source with an entirely different perspective on the behavior of houses, you can be sure that you are reading from a weak information source. So, be careful when selecting the sources.

It's great to get a reading or create your own, but the main benefit of this reading is when you put it into practice. Simply writing down what you have analyzed for yourself and putting it into a drawer isn't going to help anyone. Karmic astrology aims to improve your life, which will only happen when you take action. Even if you are fearful, you need to take the first step and make a move.

Karma repeats itself; however, you have the power to change the course of your life if you truly desire it.

Part 2: Spiritual Astrology

A Guide to the Twelve Zodiac Houses, Spirituality, Planets, Twin Flames, Soul Mates, Moon Phases, and Sun Signs

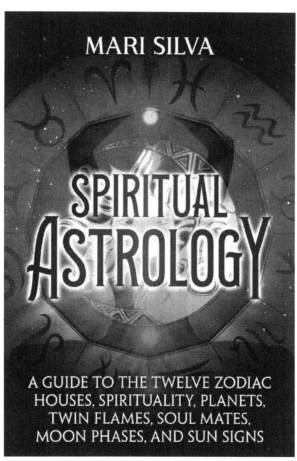

Introduction

If you're interested in knowing how astrology can help you, this book is for you. I'll explain how astrology teaches you about the past and present, the future and the present, love, career, and more.

Astrology is a wonderful tool because it's complex and deep, incorporating the motions of planets and the changing seasons, positions of the moon, your zodiac sign, and much more. All these factors culminate to give you a complete picture of yourself in time. Astrology helps you make sense of what often feels like overwhelming diverse information. As a result, you'll put things into perspective and make sound decisions truly tailored to your specific needs.

Astrology has been around for thousands of years and is widely practiced by people in many cultures. It's a form of divination, meaning it attempts to understand the movement of celestial bodies. For example, astrologers study the positions and movements of stars to predict what events might happen on Earth and when. Many people believe astrology helps them predict their future (there's a good reason for this, as you'll soon discover), so it is a helpful tool to help you with decision-making.

This book is written in simple English, so it is easy to understand, unlike many other books on the subject. You won't be left scratching your head about the concepts in this book. It is chock full of the information you're bound to find useful, whether you've studied astrology for a while or are new to the topic. So, let's dive in if you're ready to take charge of your destiny and finally find your true purpose in life.

Chapter 1: Spiritual Astrology 101

What Does Spiritual Mean?

To understand spiritual astrology, we must look at the two words that embody this concept- spiritual and astrology. What does "spiritual" mean? It refers to everything to do with the essence of life and all beings. Everything in our observable world is based on an energetic, nonphysical template known as spirit. Some people think of it as being dark matter. It is essential to note that there is more to this world than meets the eye. If you hope to understand what makes things happen the way they do, you must look past what you see and into the world beyond. I refer to the world of energy, the psychic and divine world from which every being and thing derives its existence.

What Is Astrology?

Signs.
https://pixabav.com/images/id-96309/

Astrology is the study of celestial bodies and how they affect us. The way the planets move and are positioned has a very real, perceivable effect on us. For instance, take the moon. When it's full, most of us observe odd behavior. This is no accident. Similarly, just as the moon affects us, so do other celestial bodies.

Putting It Together

So, let's talk about spiritual astrology. What does it mean? It's the study of the spiritual influences of the celestial bodies on our way of life. It determines how the placement of the planets affects everything from our careers to finances, relationships, and even health. This field of study aims to help you become more aware of the unseen strings being pulled by these influences and how you can work in tandem with them to live a rewarding life. The goal of the spiritual astrologer is to help you figure out your life path so that you can blossom and enjoy it.

As Henri J. M. Nouwen said, "*The spiritual life does not remove us from the world but leads us deeper into it.*" In other words, while looking into spiritual astrology seems an "otherworldly" endeavor that seems pointless to some people, the truth is that it will connect you with your world more strongly and give you an idea of your purpose. Far too many people live without knowing why they're here, and you can tell because they walk around with slouched shoulders and mopey faces on a path that isn't theirs.

You and Your Path

When you figure out what messages the spirit has for you through your astrological chart, you'll find clear pointers showing you what phase of life you're in and how best to work with it. For instance, you know it's time for some radical transformation when you've got a Pluto Sun transit happening, depending on whether it's opposite, square, or conjunct to your natal sun. The spirit of Pluto calls for development and growth, so this could play out in the best or worst of ways, like a new relationship, or the end of one, a job loss, health issues, or similar transitionary phases.

For most people, this is scary, especially when they don't see it for what it is. When you have many desires you'd like to manifest, the old must make way for the new. Sometimes, the only way for that to happen is through radical change, and, on the surface, it could seem rather a rough path to take.

When working with spiritual astrology, it doesn't mean that your life cannot change or you cannot craft it the way you want to because you're doomed to the spiritual energies of the stars in the sky. On the contrary, as you become a conscious co-creator of your life, knowing about the stars will help you create the life you want. It's easy to live life purposefully and powerfully when connected to the stars' energies.

Why Are You Here?

Even the best of us must wonder why we are on this little blue dot at some point in life. It doesn't take too much to notice that the world is in desperate need of healing. However, it can be incredibly difficult to figure out how to bring that healing about in a way that truly makes our souls sing.

Thankfully, this is not something you have to continue scratching your head over because you can work with the ancient wisdom embodied in the stars to find your path. In this book, you'll find your road map and discover how to use your one-of-a-kind skills and gifts to leave an indelible mark on the world forever. At present, you're possibly working in a thankless, boring job you know you're not fit for, or you're considering striking off and doing your own thing. You may even be at retirement, contemplating the next steps in life because you don't intend to remain idle. Whatever stage you're at, you can find the answer in the stars and planets. They will tell you what you can do with your time and resources to fulfill your dreams and bring back the meaning and joy you experienced as a child.

Perhaps another point that needs to be made is that "no one is an island." In other words, life is set up so that we have no choice but to have relationships with one another, whether they're personal or professional, casual or deep. You simply must relate to others. Sometimes, the process is messy, especially since humans are complex people with so many layers of emotions and thought patterns. So, as you work with the planets, you'll determine where you stand concerning other people around you. You'll learn about your desires and dreams and what others yearn for. You'll understand people on a level so deep it can only be described as "*soul-deep*." Combined with the knowledge you learn about yourself from the planets, you'll also learn your place among others and how best to work with them to achieve the best outcomes.

Your Calling: More than Just Work

It's a sad state of affairs that, for the most part, most of us merely "accept the hand we're dealt" without pausing to get in touch with our authentic selves. We fall into these roles society has picked out for us, knowing fully on the inside that we are meant for so much more. It is how we become stuck in draining relationships, situations that suck the life out of us, and jobs we hate. We do this because it is easier to get stuck in a rut or continue saying "yes" to bosses, friends, and others, even when we die a little each time we acquiesce to their demands. We justify this in so many ways, but we know we're not honoring our calling. What is that? It is whatever you truly want the most in your heart.

We all have a true calling we were sent onto this Earth to accomplish. It's what your soul is supposed to do and considers your natural gifts and the things that bring you joy and fulfillment, emotionally and spiritually. It's the key to your ultimate success in life precisely because it is the perfect blend of your dreams, drive, and gifts. Hence, it is why spiritual astrology is so important. Think of it as being plopped down in the middle of a great, big city. You want to go to the Everton Hotel, but how do you know how to get there when you don't even know where you are, let alone what roads to take? You need a map and a sense of direction. This is what your astrological chart offers you.

This natal chart will map out your entire life and contains the solar system's state as related to when and where you were born. Your birth date and time are crucial because they're not random. Your soul chose them on purpose because they intended to express themselves specifically in your present incarnation. Your chart is the blueprint to understanding your essence. Ultimately, we all have the same goal; to fully embody who we truly are. The chart uses the gifts we've been blessed with while doing our best to work around the obstacles naturally to see our life's mission through to completion.

Now is as good a time as any to clarify that your career is not necessarily the same thing as you're calling. The reality of the world we live in is that to be able to afford things, you must have a job. So we spend every second of every day of our lives thinking about work or working and don't pay much attention to what's happening spiritually or personally. In other words, we become sellouts for the sweet, sweet nectar of capitalism — money. If you think about it, money is not necessarily the goal. It's purely about the freedom it can bring you. So we continue to work hard, slaving away day and night while, paradoxically, the freedom we labor for never happens. Things are set up to have just enough money to feed yourself and stay alive long enough to go to work the next day, but no more than that. That is not freedom.

We are so wired to focus on the process of making a living that we do not consider that there are other aspects to being human. We don't think of our personal and spiritual lives as priorities but as luxuries. In other words, instead of spending time with loved ones connecting, bonding, and forming meaningful memories, it's more important to take that time to eke out another dollar. It's such a sad state of affairs, and few of us realize that we cannot take our possessions with us when we pass on. There isn't one person on their deathbed who was busy thinking about how much money they had managed to accrue in their bank account. Yet, for the most part, we do not think about this. We continue to live as though tomorrow is a given, and there will always be time until we realize we've committed most of our lives to all the wrong priorities one day.

So, here and now, dear reader, I call on you to take stock of what you've been doing so far and ask yourself, is this what you see yourself doing until the day you die? Don't you think your life could be something grander? Think about the fact that your career makes up at least 60 percent of your entire existence, and realize how great it would be to make your career line up with your soul's highest goals. Do you want to give the best of your day slaving away for something you do not believe in? Do you want to spend every last drop of blood, sweat, and tears invested in something that does not bring you joy or fulfillment? I want to believe your answer is a strong and vehement "no."

Soul's Blueprint vs. Status Quo

The argument that we should continue doing things the way we do them because "That's just the way things are" is flawed. Not everybody is fortunate enough to realize the game is rigged unfairly, that you do not have to play the game at all but could create a fulfilling life that's good for your heart. Deciding to focus on what makes your heart sing rather than sell out for a paycheck can be incredibly daunting. But I put it to you today that this is far more important than anything else you could strive for in life. Discovering your true calling and following it until the end is far more important than any degree or job position you could ever hold.

A good first step in the right direction is to get in touch with your intuition on what is right for you. For instance, when you were asked to take on more than you could handle, you could check in with your intuition whether this is a good time to say yes or no. You can also ask yourself, "Why am I here, and how can I accomplish what I'm here for?" The truth is, you can only find what you were looking for. The fact that you chose this book rather than any other, dear reader, tells me you're ready to break free of the shackles holding you back. You're ready to step into your own, and I must applaud you.

Understand that you must know who you are first and be in touch with your gut feelings before realizing the true success that has remained elusive to you all this time. Doubtless, you understand that success is not about how much money you have in your bank account. Indeed, you cannot claim to be successful if you do not enjoy what you are doing. True success is finding and following your calling, which will inevitably support you financially and spiritually (spiritual support being more important here). Aligning yourself with your spiritual cause is far more meaningful

AQUACADABRA

Many thanks for your purchase

We hope that you are 100% happy with your purchase but
if for whatever reason you are not, please contact us at
sales@aquacadabra.com
so we can hopefully resolve the problem.

If after contacting us you are still unhappy, you can
open a return or resolution case. Contacting us first will help
speed up the process, to deal with the issue quicker.

Many thanks for your custom, we look forward
to your business in the future.

The Aquacadabra Team

RETURNS FORM

Please fill in the form below, this will enable a swift return solution
THIS FORM MUST BE COMPLETED AND INCLUDED IN THE RETURNS PARCEL
Please also obtain a proof of postage certificate from the post office

Customer Information

Full Name

User Name

Delivery Address

Postcode

Phone Number

**If you selected click and collect from Argos,
please provide the Argos postcode**

Order Information

Order Date

Number/User ID

Please tick ✓ where applicable

Why are you returning your purchase?

Arrived Damaged ☐   Wrong Item Received ☐

Bought in Error ☐   Unwanted ☐   Faulty ☐

Other (Please state your reasons below)

Where did you make your purchase?

Website ☐   Phone Order ☐   Amazon ☐   Ebay ☐   ONBUY ☐

*If bought on Ebay or Amazon, have you opened a return case?
Yes ☐   No ☐

How would you like to resolve the issue?

Refund ☐   Exchange ☐

Feel free to contact us anytime concerning the status of the return.
Thank you for choosing us for your pond and aquarium needs.

than any accolades, awards, certificates, or honors that anyone else can bestow upon you for following a path that is not your own. When you decide you're going after your calling, you create significant changes in the world for the good of one and all, which counts.

Chapter 2: Sun Signs — Personality

"What's your sign?" often gets answered with a sun sign because few people know more about this ancient divination method than simply the sun sign. Let's focus on sun signs before getting into the other aspects of understanding your astrological roots.

Your sun sign is the one that tells you the truth about who you are. It's the representation of the sign the sun happened to be in when you were born. This sign gives you intricate details of who you are, making it easier to work with your strengths and weaknesses to create your desired life outcomes.

Think of your sun sign as being the very essence of your life. It is what drives you — and all astrology, too, because the other planets and celestial bodies need the sun to orbit around it. You can find this symbol on your astrology chart as a dot with a circle around it. The sun sign isn't the be-all and end-all of your chart, but it's the central focus around the other elements that affect you. It colors the way you see life.

When finding your true path in life, the only way to achieve total satisfaction and harmony is to do things the way you want to, attaining freedom, growth, and joy congruent with your inner being's desires. You can use your sun sign to piece together the puzzle of why you're here. Many of us go about the process backward, forcing ourselves to fit into containers that were never meant for us instead of choosing to be expansive and daring enough to go after that which is ours. Then, we get worked up when we find that nothing we do is good enough despite our best intentions.

It is also terrifying to allow ourselves to be our best versions because we're scared of rejection. Furthermore, many of us struggle with beliefs that put us in a cage. Society places some of these beliefs upon us, while others are of our own making. With your sun sign, you can shine a light on the way your soul chose to represent you in life so that you can be true to your path and express yourself with no fear or limitation.

A Quick Note about Dates

You should know that you must consider that what you see in the papers or on various websites with zodiac signs is usually very inaccurate. A certain date can be one sign in one year and another in a different year because each day, the sun moves through the astrological wheel a bit more than a degree, resulting in each year there could be a change in the dates. So you could easily be born right on a cusp, between two signs. The only way to tell for sure is to look at your astrology chart. Here are the 12 zodiac signs:

- Aries
- Taurus
- Gemini
- Cancer
- Leo
- Virgo
- Libra
- Scorpio
- Sagittarius
- Capricorn
- Aquarius
- Pisces

Modality

The zodiac signs fall under one of three modalities and deal with the way their lives or approaches differ:

- Cardinal — Aries, Cancer, Libra, Capricorn
- Fixed — Taurus, Leo, Scorpio, Aquarius
- Mutable — Gemini, Virgo, Sagittarius, Pisces

Cardinal signs are born leaders, always initiating things and willing to encourage change and transformation. Fixed signs are firm in all they do. They persevere no matter what, and their focus is unlike anyone else's. The mutable signs are the most adaptable. Regardless of what you throw at them, they are flexible, and it is this trait that makes them some of the most resilient people you'll ever meet.

Elements

Zodiac signs are also connected to the four classical elements — earth, water, air, and fire.

- Earth signs — Taurus, Virgo, Capricorn
- Water signs — Pisces, Cancer, Scorpio
- Air signs — Libra, Aquarius, Gemini
- Fire signs — Aries, Sagittarius, Leo

Earth signs are cautious, but that shouldn't be interpreted negatively. They think before they act. They are some of the most productive people you'll meet in life, and are quite materialistic (in a good way), meaning you can trust they will do everything they can to ensure all relevant needs are taken care of, including the state of nature. They see things as they are and are great at ensuring things aren't just started but seen through to completion. People with earth signs are also pretty sensuous.

Water signs are all about their emotions and are very aware. They are some of the most sensitive people you'll meet, very in touch with how they feel. Their intuition is off the charts, and they're usually empaths. They're also very interested in spiritual matters and vulnerable — which can be a strength in the right circumstances.

Air signs are very intellectual people. They are about being social and some of the brightest minds you'll ever encounter. They are fascinated by life, curious about everything, and always gathering information like it's running out. They love to test different ideas and enjoy rubbing their minds with others. Conversation and communication are important to them.

Fire signs are full of desire and explosive, creative power. They are some of the most restless people you'll meet because they feel the need to do more, be more, and have more. They're not particularly patient and don't do well with limits, so they ironically burn out from all that fire. However, you can rely on them to bring energy and fun into the room and make things more interesting.

Considering the Planets

Each planet has its unique energy that affects each sign differently. Before we go over each one, let's link each zodiac sign to its ruling planet:

- Aries — Mars
- Taurus — Venus
- Gemini — Mercury
- Cancer — Moon
- Leo — Sun
- Virgo — Mercury
- Libra — Venus
- Scorpio — Pluto (according to modern astrology), Mars (according to traditional astrology)
- Sagittarius — Jupiter
- Capricorn — Saturn
- Aquarius — Uranus (according to modern astrology), Saturn (according to traditional astrology)
- Pisces — Neptune (according to modern astrology), Jupiter (according to traditional astrology)

Now let's look at the effect of each celestial body.

The Sun: This is the ruler of all things, and it is an energizer. It drives everything we are at our core, so when we embrace our sun sign, we feel happy and content with life. The sun is in charge of your true purpose, creativity, conscious mind, masculine energy, and sense of self.

The Moon: The sign associated with the moon changes every 2.5 days, so it's possible to find Cancers are ruled by or connected to any of the other signs born in the same year. The moon is all about emotions and sensitivity. It is where you get the empathetic aspect of yourself, and the emotions it is tied to are the ones we have trouble expressing. It represents our shadow side, which we are only vulnerable enough to reveal to those we feel safe with. It rules feminine energy, all emotions, and instincts.

Mercury: There's more to this planet than it's in retrograde, which everyone and their grandma like to blame for their bad choices. However, there's more to this planet than flipping your life upside down. It's in charge of your intellect, sense of timing, communication style, how you reason and express yourself, and how you juggle several different conversations and lines of thought at once. It's also all about traveling and sharing information.

Venus: This planet, like the goddess, is all about love and pleasure. It's about romance and beauty in all things. Those under its influence have a great sense of aesthetics. This planet is also connected to money — especially what we spend on things that make our hearts sing. It's about sensuality and luxury in all its forms.

Mars: This planet is about tempers, aggression, how you take action, and your sexual drive. The energy of this planet is very unrefined, but this is a good thing in the right context. It's about how one asserts their dominance, goes after their goals, and deals with their libido. It's not the red planet for nothing, red being the color of passion, fire, and intensity. This planet drives our primal desires.

Jupiter: This planet rules positivity and optimism. It's in charge of good luck, abundance, and true growth. When you have this planet influencing your life, you'll likely experience amazing benefits. It's about travel and the exploration of philosophy through learning and teaching. It asks you to become more expansive by learning from life, books, and spirituality. It's the planet that inspires you to go after your grandest ideas.

Saturn: Think of this planet as the dad energy to the moon's mom energy. This strict planet is about discipline, love expressed in tough situations, drawing boundaries, and angst. Its energy could represent a challenge, but it will help you evolve into more of who you truly are and learn to take more responsibility in your life. It's about hard work and persevering to overcome your challenges.

Uranus: This planet is about upsetting the status quo and breaking away from ruts. It's all about progress, thinking outside the box, and creativity. The trouble with this planet is that it is very hard to predict what comes next. It's not a planet that cares for nostalgia. Innovation is the game's name and often smacks us in the face with profound, sudden inspiration. It's a good kind of unpredictability. Think of it as the planet of revelation and awakening.

Neptune: Neptune is the planet that rules all things ethereal. It's about your intuition and dreams, and psychic abilities. It influences your ability to connect with the spiritual and express those aspects through art. This planet is also about escapism since it is the furthest from the physical reality we know, and it's what influences our desire to run away from the harsh realities of life. Working consciously with its energies will help you become more sensitive to your spiritual side.

Pluto: Pluto rules the subconscious mind and the underworld. It is connected to great changes. This planet's energy is rather dark and heavy, and it handles the transitions from day to night, darkness to light, and endings to beginnings and back. Regardless of the spectrum, it's in charge of extremes and everything beneath the mind and heart's surface.

Now you know the planets and their effects, let's move on to the sun signs.

Sun Signs

Aries — The Ram (March 20 to April 18)

Aries sign.
Bruce The Deus, CC BY-SA 4.0 <https://creativecommons.org/licenses/by-sa/4.0>, via Wikimedia Commons: https://commons.wikimedia.org/wiki/File:Deus_Aries.png

This sign is full of spirit. People born under this sign happen to be some of the frankest and most straightforward people you'll ever meet. They have the courage that defies logic, just like the ram, and are not afraid to start new things. The essence of this sign is fresh starts, and little wonder that it happens to be the first sign. If this is you, your ruling planet is Mars, the god of war to the ancient Romans. Mars makes you a person full of desire and anger. It also imbues you with energy and a desire to take concrete action. People with Mars influences are assertive and unafraid to state what they think or want.

Symbol: The symbol of this sign is reminiscent of a ram's head, with its long face and curvy horns. It also brings to mind the idea of a fountain with water springing forth on either side. The ram is a stubborn creature that will tenaciously see what it wants and go after it. The same can be said of Aries people.

Strengths: The great thing about you, Aries, is that you are quite a formidable force to be reckoned with. No one could ever accuse you of not being bold and going after what you want with a tenacity of equal parts admired and envied. You have quite an exhilarating energy around you. Whatever your attention, you are very enthusiastic about it. You can't be considered a true individual who is unafraid of being authentic. You know who you are, and you are the least likely to allow other people to dictate how you should be.

You don't waste time figuring things out because action and progress are the same things to you. You have no trouble speaking up for what you truly believe in, even though your opinion may be at odds with what the world thinks. So, you make an excellent leader indeed. You're not afraid to take necessary risks, and you're often the first person to try new things.

Weaknesses: You tend to think of yourself a little too much and too often, and, for you, it's, "My way or the highway." You can get very competitive in a bad way, to the point where you don't care who you hurt or sacrifice in the process. You're so eager for what you want that you see rules and actively think of ways to break them to obtain what you want — and, of course, this doesn't always work out well for you.

Sure, you're very passionate about several things, but the trouble is that you don't settle down long enough to see all of them through, and, as a result, you find that your initial spark dies out. When it comes to your emotions, it's not easy for you to put yourself in another person's shoes, making people think you're very insensitive. Additionally, it takes very little to get you to blow your lid. Thankfully, your anger is over as quickly as it sets in, but that doesn't make it less scary.

Famous Aries People: Reese Witherspoon, Sarah Jessica Parker, Kiera Knightley, Elton John, Jonathan Groff, Fergie, Mariah Carey, Quentin Tarantino, Ewan McGregor, Jonathan Van Ness, Alec Baldwin, and Robert Downey Jr.

Taurus — The Bull (April 19 to May 20)

Taurus.

There's no one as dependable as you, Taurus. You're the person who will stick around through thick and thin. You also love to enjoy yourself, and you're given pleasure since Venus rules you. Like the bull, you have stamina, unlike others. You're the person who is comfortable with taking on responsibility and one of the more loyal and devoted signs.

Symbol: The glyph for this sign looks like a bull's head, a circle with two horns on top of it. It is also reminiscent of a woman's womb with its fallopian tubes.

Strengths: You're the one who takes the Aries energy and grounds it, in reality, to be applied to practical matters that bring forth actual results. Security matters to you in all ways, so you're very cautious about making hasty decisions. You're the sort to hold on fiercely, and when you've decided something, no one can change your mind. Tenacious is your name, and you accomplish your goals by remaining determined, no matter how long it takes. You're gentle, kind, a romantic, and a lover of all things sensual. You also love beauty and look for ways to bring it to life in your environment.

Weaknesses: You take your time with things, which is usually a struggle for others to deal with. You're likely to find yourself stuck in a groove, and on top of that, you're beyond stubborn. When applied to your morals or goals, it's a good thing, but it also means you're resistant to change even when it would be good for you. You can hold on to old ways of doing things even at the cost of your own joy. You can also get greedy and jealous and engage in quite the pity party for yourself. Sometimes you're insensitive and possessive and have no qualms exploiting people. You don't get mad like Aries, but everyone in your path will feel it when you do.

Famous Taurus People: Jack Nicholson, Harry S. Truman, Mark Zuckerberg, Dwayne Johnson, Che Guevara, Adolf Hitler, Stevie Wonder, Kirsten Dunst, Tina Fey, and Adele.

Gemini – The Twins (May 21 to June 20)

Gemini.
https://pixabay.com/es/illustrations/geminis-astrolog%c3%ada-hor%c3%b3scopo-2782077/

You're bright. You have a way with your words, and you can persuade the Saudis to buy sand. This is due to Mercury's influence on you. You're a very lively person to engage with and agile too.

Symbol: Gemini's glyph resembles two pillars, or the number eleven, with curved lines connecting them at the top and bottom, facing outward. They represent the two sides of this person.

Strengths: You're always in touch with your inner child, happy and gregarious. Your intelligence knows no bounds and is further boosted by your thirst for knowledge. Nothing excites you more than new people, the latest news, and new things. You're the type of person who probably has more than one job simultaneously. You probably have more than one book you're reading right now and more than one lover. Spontaneity is very important to you. Sure, you may commit yourself to many things at once and complain about it, but the truth is you love it.

Weaknesses: The downside of being a Gemini is that you are hyperactive and cannot focus. You care more about instant gratification rather than taking your time with things. Your attention span is very short, which causes you trouble more often than not. Sitting still isn't something you do well. As much as you get excited about things, you talk yourself out of them with equal energy. Other people may find your intense fascination with them a bit of a drain. Your worst traits are superficiality and deceit, and some people will say you're full of hot air and have no depth to you emotionally. You're the sort of person who would rather adapt to a bad situation than do something about it, and you may even rewrite the situation to suit yourself. All consequences can be dealt with — just much, much later.

Famous Gemini People: Donald Trump, Angeline Jolie, Nicole Kidman, Arthur Conan Doyle, Marilyn Monroe, Prince, Kanye West, Allen Ginsberg, Anne Frank, Queen Victoria, John F. Kennedy, Aaron Sorkin, Salmon Rushdie, Alanis Morrissette, and Kendrick Lamar.

Cancer — The Crab (June 21 to July 22)

Cancer.

Being ruled by the moon makes you very in touch with your intuition if you're a Cancer. You look within yourself a lot and are very aware of your emotions. You're security conscious, too. While you may sometimes feel like an emotional mess, there's more to you than that, and you don't allow your vulnerabilities to get in the way of attaining your desires.

Symbol: The cancer glyph is reminiscent of the yin yang symbol, the numbers 6 and 9, with their curved tails on the top and bottom, respectively, while the circles are side by side. The symbol is also said to represent the breasts and the fluidity of emotions.

Strengths: Due to the water element, you have no trouble allowing your emotions to be open, and, at the same time, you are deeply reflective. You have ambition and are deeply connected to the world around you, making your moods go up and down when combined with your emotions. You can be as shrewd as you need to be, trusting your emotions and intuition to guide you through all situations. You're connected to your past and history and love nothing more than family and a sense of belonging.

You're a supportive friend, very loyal, and rather affectionate, and never give up on the people you care about. Regardless of how you feel, you ensure that your goals are attained. Even when your journey toward your goal causes you to cry, you continue to put one foot in front of the other.

Weaknesses: You appear tough on the outside, but you're also soft on the inside like a crab. When something scares you, you tuck yourself back into your shell. You're not a person to deal with issues head-on. However, you'll stick up for yourself when you need to, but usually wind up putting your foot in it and then go into denial about the truth, making it hard for others to connect with you. You will inevitably overcome powerful emotions because of the moon, which means that sometimes you won't deal with them well. Your fear of being abandoned or having no resources to fall back on makes you fiercely hold on to things that you need to let go of.

Famous Cancer People: The Dalai Lama, Ariana Grande, Nelson Mandela, Kevin Bacon, Wendy Williams, Pablo Neruda, Florence Ballard, Chiwetel Ejiofor, Priyanka Chopra, Kevin Hart, Khloe Kardashian, Mindy Kaling, Alan Turing, Mike Tyson, and Robin Williams.

Leo — The Lion (July 23 to August 22)

Leo.

You're one of the friendliest people anyone will ever meet as a Leo. You collect friends like the Kardashians collect plastic surgeons. You're a very warm person, and people love to be around you because you're so outgoing and how good you make them feel. It also doesn't hurt that in everything you do, you demonstrate flair.

Symbol: The glyph of this sign looks like a circle with a tail that swirls out of it, just like a lion's tail.

Strengths: You're friendly, joyful, and loyal to a fault. You go after what you want with passion, and your social life is brimming with fun activities. Your goal is to live your best life, and you do a good job of having fun with it. You are usually the entertainer in a group because, naturally, you're the center of attention, like the sun that shines. Your sense of humor is amazing, and you know how to share the best of yourself even when others can't find theirs. Charisma is your name, a fact you know and are proud of. You love luxury, respect, and honor. You enjoy glamor, consider yourself royalty, and are willing to put in the work. You're also generous.

Weaknesses: You have trouble letting people know just how vulnerable you are. You can be quite the people-pleaser because you want to be liked, so you speak for people's approval instead of your truth. In other words, you are quite at home, lying and manipulating others. Sure, your intentions are pure because you don't want to hurt people, but this isn't the way to do things. You're not a person to be silenced for long, and eventually, you'll let the truth out — even if you might exaggerate a bit. Your worst traits are being vain, overly dramatic, and controlling. However, you're hardly ever at your worst, so you don't have to worry too much about that. The acknowledgment you seek will come to you naturally when you relinquish your need to control and just be your bright, sunny self.

Famous Leo People: J. K. Rowling, Charlize Theron, Alfred Hitchcock, Carl Jung, Robert De Niro, Madonna, Mick Jagger, Andy Warhol, Steve Martin, Neil Armstrong, Fidel Castro, Usain Bolt, Sandra Bullock, and Viola Davis.

Virgo — The Virgin (August 23 to September 22)

Virgo.

There's no mind sharper than a Virgo. You have Mercury to thank for your quick wit and communication skills. You're a person who sees what most others don't, and your level of insight is unmatched. You're also rather articulate and critical. People may whine about that, but they don't know you're more critical of yourself than anyone or anything else. You don't believe in being perfect, so you constantly want to improve yourself.

Symbol: The glyph of Virgo looks like the letter M, with an extra "prong" that crosses over the bottom of the third one. It's a sign representing the female genitalia.

Strengths: No one can put one over you because you see the devil in the details. You're efficient, can read between the lines, and glean what's not being said and what is meant. You're funny, smart, and can hold a conversation very well. You're very analytical, think clearly, and concentrate better than most. You love to learn "new things." Yet, despite all you know, you're a modest person, making you rather attractive. No one knows better than you that you're not perfect, but you know you'll always strive to be better. The difference between you and the other earth signs is your efficiency. Discipline and organization are your wheelhouses, and there is no limit. You won't push to become who you want to be and are open to helping other people. Sometimes you help them to the point of disregarding your own needs. However, it is no shock since Virgo is the sign of service.

Weaknesses: You need to go easy on people — meaning yourself, too. Sometimes, you can't distinguish between what's just okay and a grand idea. When what you want doesn't happen, your disappointment knows no bounds and can bring you down to the point of depression. While you may play the martyr to uplift other people, you struggle deeply with anxiety, shyness, and not belonging or inferiority. You struggle with guilt and worry about many things, even what isn't yours to be concerned about.

Famous Virgo People: Beyonce Knowles, George R. R. Martin, Dave Chapelle, Amy Poehler, Sean Connery, Ivan the Terrible, Agatha Christie, Stephen King, Amy Winehouse, Warren Buffet, Louis C. K., Sophia Loren, and Michael Jackson.

Libra — The Scales (September 23 to October 22)

Libra.

You are one of the most rational people on the planet, Libra. You love all things beautiful, you adore love, and you're an exceptionally fair person, making it easy to hang out with you. You're all about being civilized and proper.

Symbol: The glyph looks like the equal sign, with the top dash curving upwards in the middle. This represents justice and the sun setting on the horizon.

Strengths: You're refined in all your ways, and, additionally, you're the definition of cool. Your temper is balanced. You notice things and were born a diplomat. You want nothing more than peace wherever you are and have a deep appreciation for music, art, and aesthetically pleasing things. You're an easygoing person with a charm that draws many to you. You're also quite a flirt, but that doesn't mean you're not loyal in your relationships. Your intellect is excellent, and you're sensible in all you do. You're a person who wants to hear all sides of the story before drawing your conclusions. Hence, you love debating, doing your best to be objective, and balancing your emotions with careful logic.

Weaknesses: You let people make you feel like you're not worthy, worry a lot, and when you don't know who you are, you lack confidence. You are very critical of yourself, especially if some of your planets are placed in Virgo. You're anxious about making a good impression and doing everything to make people happy, which doesn't always work out well. On the flip side, sometimes you don't do as much as you should. When you don't feel great, you crawl into your shell, choosing to be vague and indulging yourself only. You don't do well with squabbles, yet you don't have a problem causing them. You seek balance in your life but don't do well keeping it. Your tendency to overanalyze things can be problematic when deciding on something important.

Famous Libra People: F. Scott Fitzgerald, Cardi B, Gwyneth Paltrow, Gwen Stefani, Mahatma Gandhi, Kate Winslet, Brie Larson, Kim Kardashian, Eminem, Matt Damon, Friedrich Nietzsche, Ralph Lauren, Oscar Wilde, Neil deGrasse Tyson, and Will Smith.

Scorpio — The Scorpion (October 23 to November 21)

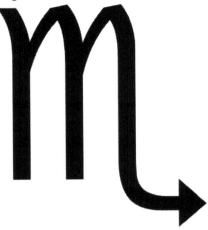

Scorpio.

This sign is all about intensity. You're ruled by Pluto, making you a very extreme and interesting person. You're not afraid to take a walk on the wild side.

Symbol: The glyph is the letter M with a tail at the end of the third prong, representing the scorpion's tail.

Strengths: You're a magnetic person with a deep passion for everything you do. Your sensuality and vibrancy are enthralling. You're a complex person who takes life into your own hands, and you tend to do what you want, which makes you interesting. You're in tune with body language, words, love drama, and drawn to all things mysterious. Your mood goes from heavenly highs to hellish lows because you feel everything deeply. You love your privacy, but you're very good at getting others to open up to you about their dark secrets. Your willpower and self-control are worth commending, and you always execute your plans at the right time, not a moment before or after.

Weaknesses: You have some of the nastiest traits, so watch out for them. You're manipulative, quite adept at lying, and arrogant. You keep secrets to lord them over others or manipulate them. When you have no other options, you have no qualms about hurting people deeply, and you are horrible at forgiving people. You can be very cold, full of spite and jealousy at your worst. For the most part, Scorpios do well at not letting that dark part get the better of them, and they struggle with a lot of depression.

Famous Scorpios: Bill Gates, Joe Biden, Roseanne Barr, Drake, Julia Roberts, Leonardo DiCaprio, RuPaul, Kelly Osbourne, Jonas Salk, Albert Camus, Robert F. Kennedy, Neil Young, Matthew McConaughey, and Caitlyn Jenner.

Sagittarius — The Archer (November 22 to December 21)

Sagittarius.
https://pixabay.com/es/vectors/sagitario-zod%c3%adaco-se%c3%b1ales-36395/

You're full of energy, and you're your own person and ruled by Jupiter. Your mind is always full of possibilities, and you love nothing more than to explore all of life through travel and new people with new ideas.

Symbol: This glyph is an arrow pointing upward and to the right, with a dash going through the bottom of the arrow, making it look like a cross. It is the centaur's arrow and represents lofty goals.

Strengths: You're a cheerful soul and love to wander. You have amazing wit and are always ready for some excitement. You're fun to have as a friend and think about the deep things of life with those you care about. You think life is about growing in wisdom and experience, and you don't care to hold yourself back for the sake of security. You don't do well being restricted, and you'd rather be your own person. You're open-minded, easy to get along with, and spontaneous. You're fearless in your approach and passionate about religion and philosophy.

Weaknesses: While you love to have a good time, an aspect of you wants nothing more than to grow mentally, and this makes you flounder. You're not the most organized person and sometimes very impractical. You aren't careful with your money and are not the most reliable person, making promises you could never hope to keep. Also, you're the most tactless sign. You don't know how to tell the truth with love and blurt things out before you know it. Other times, your silence gives you away.

Famous Sagittarius People: Mark Twain, Frank Sinatra, Sarah Paulson, Sarah Silverman, Jon Stewart, Steven Spielberg, Jane Austen, Zoe Kravitz, Winston Churchill, William Blake, Tiffany Haddish, Lucy Liu, and Pablo Escobar.

Capricorn — The Goat (December 22 to January 19)

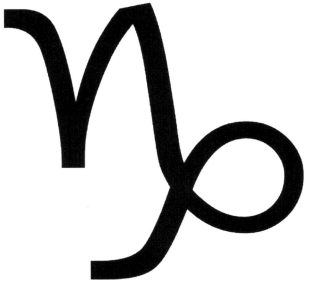

Capricorn.

You love tradition, and if there's anyone who's a stickler for the rules, it's you. You love rules because you thrive with them.

Symbol: This glyph resembles a combination of numbers 7 and 6, showing you the goat's horns.

Strengths: You love competition and are very productive. You could never be accused of being immature. Even when you were a kid, you were a rather serious person, which most of your peers didn't understand. As an adult, you come into your own and have learned to be a happier person. You have ambition for days and are patient while achieving your goals, no matter how far away they may seem. You don't have a problem with other people's needs and will also help them achieve their goals. You're calm in the face of trouble and know how to discipline yourself without going to the extreme. You carry a natural air of dignity and authority. You're also sensual, like the other earth signs.

Weaknesses: You're quite conservative, so you don't do things spontaneously. You worry about money and how you're perceived, and, at your worst, you're quite the pessimist. You repress your real self because you're worried about being judged. You don't know how to relax because you feel you always have to be on the go and there's so much still to do. You sense that you'd do much more if you could be alone. You tend to work too hard, and even now, as you read this, you think it's a good thing to be proud of. However, it's vital to relax. Also, you're not good with feelings because you don't like to show people how vulnerable you are or how much you're hurting. It would serve you to deal with the truth as it is.

Famous Capricorn People: Carlos Castaneda, Shona Rhimes, Jim Carrey, Haruki Murakami, Kate Middleton, David Bowie, Dolly Parton, Christian Louboutin, Orlando Bloom, John Legend, Zooey Deschanel, Muhammed Ali, Denzel Washington, Martin Luther King, and J. R. R. Tolkien.

Aquarius — The Water Bearer (January 20 to February 18)

Aquarius.

You're a person considered original, all about your future and how to make progress. You gain insight into many things, and you're peculiar.

Symbol: The glyph is two zigzagging lines stacked on top of each other, representing water waves or light.

Strengths: You're a true humanitarian, theoretically speaking. Your principles are very benevolent, and you do your best to live by them. For you, everyone is equal and should be treated that way, so it bothers you when you see things to the contrary. You love to create things, technology, and all things science. Your finger is always on the world's pulse, and the stranger and more unconventional, the better. You're warm and full of charisma and make friends with people from all walks of life.

Weaknesses: Sometimes, you are very immature, refusing to get along with others. You're stubborn about ideas you hold dear, even when they don't work out well. Your altruistic viewpoint is often thought of as fake or for appearance purposes. Your actual self is often detached, and you'd rather deal with ideas, not feelings. You may appear warm and welcoming, but when people get closer, they sense you're cold, insensitive, and, ironically enough, it's easy to get under your skin. When you're at your lowest and worst, you're pretty much a robot. You're also a tad insecure, although it's not immediately obvious to everyone.

Famous Aquarius People: Sheryl Crow, Ellen DeGeneres, Oprah Winfrey, Paul Newman, Ashton Kutcher, Charles Darwin, Wolfgang Amadeus Mozart, The Weekend, Dr. Dre, Vanessa Redgrave, Paris Hilton, Michael B. Jordan, Cristiano Ronaldo, and Virginia Woolf.

Pisces — The Fish (February 19 to March 19)

Pisces.

You're all about your imagination and dreams. This sign is about everything spiritual and true compassion. Your biggest challenge is learning how to ground yourself in the world despite your penchant for wanting to escape it.

Symbol: The glyph looks like two letter Cs backing each other, connected by a dash. This represents the connection between the inner and outer worlds.

Strengths: You're sensitive, and you pick up on everything emotionally. You are rather psychic, but it's hard to stay safe because you're not the best at setting boundaries. You sense when things are off between people, which bothers you deeply. You love it when your people win and celebrate with them because your heart is big and full of compassion. Your imagination knows no bounds, and you love to daydream, which helps you with creative solutions and ideas that prove useful in life. You're open to change and have a level of faith many only hope to achieve. Even when things don't work out, you trust it was for your greater good.

Weaknesses: Sometimes, you get lost in your head. When you're at your lowest, it's easy to deceive you. You lose touch with rationality, and it's easy for people to hurt you and for life to beat you down. You are often incredibly entitled to the nth degree. You also aren't good at decision-making, and, more than anyone, you deceive yourself the most, sometimes to the point of not acknowledging your part in finding yourself where you are. When things aren't going well, you wait for someone to take care of you or save you rather than taking action. You can be full of anger, self-pity, and resentment when things don't go your way and are likely to give in to drugs and alcohol to escape yourself and your troubles.

Famous Pisces People: Albert Einstein, Rihanna, Rob Lowe, Kurt Cobain, Queen Latifah, Chelsea Handler, Trevor Noah, Ruth Bader Ginsburg, Victor Hugo, Bryan Cranston, Glenn Close, and Erykah Badu.

Chapter 3: Sun Signs — Compatibility

Your sun sign is responsible for how you see yourself and others see you. It's responsible for your sense of self-worth and confidence, but more than that, it has a strong influence on your life path. When you know what your sun sign is and how it affects you, you can further discover how your sun sign interacts with others.

What Is Compatibility?

Some sun signs are more compatible with each other than with others. If you want to know how to get along with others better in love, friendships, and at work, it's worth looking into their sun signs to see how well you are likely to get along. You shouldn't immediately assume that because someone has a sign known to be incompatible with yours, you should automatically assume you'll never get along. Regardless of their sun sign, even if they are one of the three dark personalities - Machiavellians, psychopaths, and narcissists - you should be able to get along with them when needed.

I'd like to note that the various combinations we will look at depend on other factors besides the particular sun signs, like the moon sign. So you must consider other factors besides the sun signs if you want to figure out a specific relationship. Now without further ado, let's look at each sign and how it fares with other signs.

Aries' Best Match

Leo is the one for you, Aries. Of all the signs, you won't tame this lion, and it is why you're drawn to them. You're drawn to that regal aura around them, and you love their boldness. It is an especially great combo when the Aries is a woman and the Leo is a man. Leo's going to be the one in charge here. You're both fire signs, which means you're compatible. It also means there will be a fair bit of drama, but don't worry about it because you can work your way through any trouble — usually in the bedroom. You both make each other better. Leo can learn to deal with an Aries' temper and need to fight, while Aries will have an energizing effect on Leo.

Aries' Worst Match

You and Taurus will often lock horns because you share little or nothing in common. Building a relationship together is a futile exercise. Aries is all about opportunity, taking every shot they can to do courageous things, which means stepping outside of one's comfort zone. On the other hand, Taurus only wants peace and stability as it's comforting for them, so they'll think Aries is too much work, and the latter will think the Taurus much too boring.

Taurus' Best Match

Capricorn is made for you, Taurus. You mesh well together, being earth signs and have the same thought patterns. You're grounded individuals who are always practical, and thankfully there's enough difference between your characters to give you the balance to make this union work. Taurus is quiet and enjoys peace, reveling in materialism and pleasure. When this goes too far, they are indulgent or downright lazy. Capricorn is a diligent sign, very resourceful, and always putting things in place to ensure their success. They can be quite the workaholic. Together, these signs balance each other out, with Capricorn lighting a fire under Taurus and Taurus teaching Capricorn just to chill.

Taurus' Worst Match

Sagittarius absolutely won't jive well with you. Sagittarius likes to travel and enjoys new things, while Taurus is resistant to change and prefers routine. They want nothing more than comfort, great sex, delicious food, and a comfy bed to end the day. This doesn't work for Sagittarius because they crave nothing more than travel, and that's far too chaotic for Taurus. Also, Taurus gets jealous easily, an unattractive trait to the archer, who certainly doesn't want to be possessed.

Gemini's Best Match

You would do wonderfully well with a Libra. You work well together socially and love hanging out with each other. You both are lifelong learners, making it easy for you to connect with people across all spectrums of life. You could never be bored with each other because you have loads to talk about. Gemini understands Libra's indirectness in communication because you're intuitively connected. They are both quite flirtatious and don't get jealous or insecure because they understand this about each other.

Gemini's Worst Match

Gemini has no business being in a relationship with a Scorpio. Where Gemini is happy to be involved in several things at once, Scorpio focuses on doing only one thing and giving it their all. To Gemini, that's an obsession. As for Scorpio, they see the Gemini as a shallow person. They don't find it easy to connect. Scorpio can't stand how much Gemini can change, while Gemini doesn't understand how Scorpio focuses on one thing. Gemini is a social butterfly, and Scorpio can't handle this because they're prone to jealously. Add in Gemini's propensity for flirting, which could be a problem. Also, Gemini may not always know when Scorpio doesn't want other people to know something, and it could tick the latter off when the former accidentally spills the beans.

Cancer's Best Match

Pisces and Cancer work beautifully well together, both being water signs, so the emotional bond they share is incredible. They understand each other so well that they don't even need to say a word to each other to pass a message. They know how to offer comfort and warmth to each other, and where they diverge in character, their differences are actually good for the union. Cancer is a practical sign, a homebody that loves to care for others. They can get a little too worried and nervous as a result. Pisces is a spiritual sign with a gentle soul, and they're some of the most compassionate people on Earth who understand human nature. Despite this, they're usually not grounded in reality and have issues being practical. So Pisces will learn this from Cancer, and they help Cancer find peace.

Cancer's Worst Match

Cancer would do horribly with Aquarius, assuming they even manage to find each other attractive, to begin with. Cancer comes from an emotional and intuitive place, while Aquarius is a logical person who holds reason above all else. They don't get each other, so they cannot connect, let alone make peace with what makes them different. No one can make Aquarius feel deeply, and no Cancer can change that. Cancer will find Aquarius too cold. It's rare to find a successful connection between these two.

Leo's Best Match

Besides Aries, Leo is also compatible with Libra, who is quite the diplomat, flirt, and conversationalist. Libra naturally makes Leo want to be extra charming and smooth, and they do this without threatening to snatch the limelight from the lion, making them even more attractive. They're the couple you enjoy observing. They're very social and give the best parties, with Libra as the most gracious host and Leo the center of attention. Even behind closed doors, they're like this. Now and then, it's wise for them to take a break from performing and just relax. Libra could be the cooler of the two when they're alone, but the love is still strong between the two.

Leo's Worst Match

Leo and Virgo couldn't possibly work together. They're adjacent to each other on the zodiac circle, to begin with, meaning they have trouble connecting. Sure, there are rare exceptions, but rare is the keyword. Leo loves to take center stage, while Virgo is a modest person who prefers being at home behind the scenes. Leo loves to be adored, but Virgo doesn't do so well with this, even though they appreciate sincere compliments when they count. Virgo tries to be helpful with their constructive suggestions, but this doesn't go down well with the vulnerable Leo, who feels criticized. It doesn't help that Virgo will not offer a compliment unless it is well earned.

Virgo's Best Match

Virgo and Capricorn are wonderful. They're both earth signs and practical people with a healthy sense of materialism. They do well working together and intuitively know what each other needs for support. The odds are they fell in love at work. If you're in this relationship, you both share a great sense of humor, and laughter is the norm for you two. Your mutual joy allows you to relax with each other and be more sensual. Your differences also work well together. For instance, Capricorn has little time for nonsense in their career and ambitions and always considers their future in all they do, but this makes them forget important things like health. On the other hand, Virgo sees all the details everyone else misses and reminds Capricorn to take care of themselves. Capricorn also helps Virgo when they become scattered and unfocused.

Virgo's Worst Match

Aquarius and Virgo are a no-no. These signs are intellectual but not compatible. Virgo is grounded and practical. They like to file things in the appropriate boxes. As for Aquarius, they don't care for the box, and that's the problem. However, they recognize each other's intellectual prowess, so they could work well in other ways, just not romantically. To Aquarius, Virgo fusses far too much. To Virgo, Aquarius is a rule-breaker, and not in a good way.

Libra's Best Match

Other than Leo and Gemini, Libra does well with Aquarius. As fellow air signs, they're very compatible. Libra is the social one who has no trouble fitting in anywhere. Aquarius is usually the odd one in groups. They're both turned on by intellect, and this is what pulls them to each other. Libra is intelligent, but they downplay this trait because they understand some people can't handle it. However, they know a lot about everything and can hold their own in conversations on any topic with any person. Libra is a just and fair sign, so it honors rules and follows social cues, but deep down, there's a bit of mischief that peeks out now and then, which draws them to Aquarius.

Libra's Worst Match

It could never work out between a Libra and a Scorpio. Scorpio's always spoiling for a fight, and Libra doesn't have time. Libra is a courteous person who loves honesty, peace, and harmony, all of which Scorpio struggles with. Libra will tell "white lies" for the sake of peace, but lying isn't in their nature. Scorpios values honesty too, but when they're at their worst, they can pull a complete 180 and manipulate and lie to their heart's content. This trait is rather ironic, given that they're very intuitive and can tell when they're being lied to. They're driven to get down to the bottom of things, but it unsettles Libra because the truth may not be something they can handle. Libra loves to learn about people, but they don't want to get into the dark stuff, and they're not in the mood to share this either - something Scorpio desires deeply.

Scorpio's Best Match

Scorpio and Pisces work well together, being water signs. They're both incredibly intense and sensitive to emotions. They are intuitively connected and can even share telepathy. Pisces is the more free-flowing person, while Scorpio has the drive and is more intense. Pisces is the more flexible one. Scorpio is always the leader in the relationship, being protective and in charge regardless of gender. Pisces brings their softness into the relationship to bring Scorpio the tranquility they need. Pisces's innate understanding of humans makes them one of the few signs that see past Scorpio's misbehavior, making it hard for Scorpio to hide the truth of their vulnerability. They work well in the long haul.

Scorpio's Worst Match

Other than Gemini, Sagittarius is another sign that Scorpio does not do well with. These two signs share no common traits. Scorpios want intimacy, and they want a deep relationship. This is at odds with Sagittarius's desire to be free. There's no room for negotiations here. Nothing will ever be enough for Scorpio in this pairing, and Sagittarius will feel there's a noose around their neck that grows tighter each day they spend with Scorpio. Fortunately, it's rare that these two ever connect.

Sagittarius' Best Match

Aries is the best match for the archer, and there's a lot of fire going on here. They both love to go on adventures together, and this is a relationship full of fun times. Sagittarius' love for travel is something that Aries is fine with, and Aries doesn't need Sagittarius to be emotionally over-invested in the relationship. Also, Aries respects Sagittarius, making them even more sexually attracted to the archer. They think of Sagittarians as strong people and are drawn to strength. Aries isn't the easiest person to get along with, so Sagittarius' laid-back attitude is a positive for this union. Being laid back doesn't mean the archer isn't strong, though. They're a lovely combination of relaxed and powerful, which means they can handle whatever Aries throws their way.

Sagittarius' Worst Match

Besides Scorpio and Taurus, Sagittarius doesn't do well with a fellow Sagittarius because while they may both get along, they won't remain together for the long haul. Sagittarius people are afraid of committing because it means having to settle down, the complete antithesis of their desire to explore. If they had their way, they'd be happy to live a single life until they pass away. Neither partner will be able to really drive the relationship forward because they're not inclined to settle.

Capricorn's Best Match

Capricorn goes with Virgo very well. They're both earth signs and can be with each other harmoniously. There's more tension here than you'd have with a Taurus and Capricorn pairing. In this case, Capricorn has to bring balance to the relationship. They're supportive of each other, with

Capricorn considering the long term and Virgo able to handle the short-term stuff. There is romance, but there's also work. This relationship would be even more beautiful if they got into business together.

Capricorn's Worst Match

Leo and Capricorn don't do well together because they're always competing to be on top, and they couldn't be more different. Leo exudes that regal aura, and they won't let you forget it. They have to be adored and want to be in the lead. On the flip side, you have Capricorn, who's more interested in getting things done. They couldn't care less about how cool Leo is, which infuriates the latter. Capricorn comes off as a bore to a Leo, so it's not common to find a working relationship between these two.

Aquarius' Best Match

Aquarius and Sagittarius work well together. They may seem distant, and they don't need emotional closeness, but somehow this is what makes them work. They get each other. They know what it's like to feel overwhelmed or sick of neediness from a partner, so they don't mind being with each other. They're also the couple who would love to live in their own homes, have separate bedrooms, or have an open relationship. Aquarius is aloof but friendly and quite emotionally stable, and Sagittarius brings an exciting energy to the relationship.

Aquarius' Worst Match

Aquarius wouldn't do well with a Virgo, even though they may share the same friends since they have a flair for intellectual matters and events. However, they go after their passions differently, with Virgo being all about the details and Aquarius about the big picture. Aquarius is also a rule breaker, which doesn't sit well with Virgo. These two will inevitably frustrate each other.

Pisces' Best Match

Other than Cancer, Pisces does well with Virgo. They are opposite signs, which means they work well together as partners. They're both about offering service and understanding the value of staying humble. However, they serve others differently. Where Virgo is a practical helper, Pisces is more into helping people with spiritual matters. Pisces has a better view of the bigger picture than Virgo, but they're not the best with details. However, Virgo can see the details that Pisces misses, and this is where they meet each other halfway and work wonderfully well together.

Pisces' Worst Match

Pisces and Leo do not work. They don't have enough similarities, and their differences do not complement each other. When Pisces is a man and Leo is a woman, she may have a problem seeing his strength, which is present but not the sort the Leo woman cares for. They could probably work if she could only look at him from a different perspective. The opposite is true when it's a Leo man with a Pisces woman. She'll be absolutely in love with how much of a charmer he is, and he'll love her for adoring him. However, they'll see that they don't have much in common with time.

Chapter 4: Sun Signs at Work

Each sun sign leads to a different work personality.
https://pixabay.com/images/id-2562325/

While every person has their unique individual flair, your sun sign can indeed shape aspects of your personality and work style while also providing insight into how others react to you based on your birth date. There are certain qualities that the sun sign determines when assessing individuals that are beneficial for you and your colleagues to understand.

For example, if you are an Aries, you may be described as strong-willed and confident. However, it is also common for people with this sun sign to be impatient and temperamental. These characteristics make interacting with others difficult. But if you know these potential personality struggles, you can work toward avoiding being considered difficult.

Your sun sign can give you a glimpse into your personality, but it is not the only influencing factor. When you consider your job or career path, take advantage of the insight your sign offers.

Aries at Work

The Aries sun sign is bold and outspoken. In the workplace, this means you are direct and, at times, bold with your comments or words.

Aries people are known to be competitive and determined, so working with a like-minded group of individuals will be like a game of one-upmanship. Avoid allowing yourself to be defined by your colleagues' opinions to avoid getting caught in this cycle.

In some cases, Aries leaders make insensitive comments when frustrated or annoyed with the situation. This is a trait that will cause problems if it continues. Remind yourself to take a moment and calm down before you respond to a co-worker's comment.

Strengths

- Energetic and enthusiastic
- Ambitious and confident
- Creative and energetic

Weaknesses

- Impatient and temperamental
- Dominant and demanding.

Best career choices: Stock trading, entrepreneur, advertising, media, entertainment, security, politics, sports, disaster management, emergency services.

Worst career choices: Anything that is tedious and repetitive, such as banking, cleaning, and data analysis.

Taurus at Work

The Taurus is serious and capable. The confidence Taurus brings to the table can inspire others, but it can also drive them to develop a lack of communication or otherwise unnecessary work-related arguments. The Taurus personality type is often perceived as calm, steady, and dependable, but these individuals take a moment to put themselves in other people's shoes before speaking up.

The best way for Taurus people to avoid conflicts with co-workers is to identify the feeling behind others' reactions to you. Understanding how their reactions differ from yours will help you communicate better with your colleagues and have easier interactions overall.

Those with the Taurus sun sign are known for being practical and reliable. This is good for being respected by your colleagues. But this sign is also known for being stubborn, so it is important to balance your professionalism with your need to get things done your way.

Taurus people also lean toward materialism, which means they spend as much time thinking about what they want as they think about the available possibilities. This characteristic makes them appear self-centered and impacts how Aries interacts with a Taurus.

Strengths
- Methodical and patient
- Abiding and tenacious.

Weaknesses
- Stubborn and complacent
- Materialistic and inflexible.

Best career choices: Medicine, pharmacy, art direction, interior design, accounting, banking, nursing, project management, real estate brokerage, architecture, music, cuisine, and scientific research.

Worst career choices: Jobs that require quick decision-making, like being in the police force, being a firefighter, or a trauma surgeon.

Gemini at Work

Those with the Gemini sun sign are enthusiastic, talkative, witty, versatile, and adaptive. Interacting with them is a challenge because they have an opinion on everything, making it difficult for others to get a word edgewise. To get along well with those who have your sun sign, you must be willing to listen while also offering your thoughts when necessary or appropriate.

Geminis are known for being intelligent and unorthodox. So, they will frequently challenge conventions and rules and question why they are even necessary in the first place. This can make them a welcomed addition to any team, particularly if they provide an innovative edge or creative direction to a project.

However, your colleagues may see you as a little flighty when taking criticism.

Avoid making the mistake of assuming that everyone wants the same things or appreciates your unique work style. You will question why you are there in the first place since it may feel like everyone is doing the same thing.

If you are a Gemini, it is important to take a moment before responding to a co-worker's feedback or criticism.

Strengths

- Unconventional and creative
- Able to find solutions to problems
- Brilliant and quick-witted.

Weaknesses

- Cynical and defensive
- Naive and lacking basic skills.
- Self-centered
- Sensitive

Best career choices: Diplomacy, acting, journalism, travel, blogging, event management, language translation, advertising, media, short course creation and teaching, sales, information technology management, and tour guide.

Worst career choices: Since you're not the best at committing to a single decision, you should stay away from jobs focused on long-term matters and projects. Also, if it's a job that won't let you socialize, it's not for you.

Cancer at Work

Those with the Cancer sun sign are nurturing and caring. This works well for you in the workplace since your co-workers will know how much commitment and effort you put into each project or assignment. However, you have a harder time breaking away to make new connections because of this sign's loyalty.

Cancer people can often work alone due to their affinity for privacy, so they are not always made aware of the project's progress since they miss out on opportunities for recognition and advancement. This can cause frustration when they do not receive the same attention as others. Ensure everyone is involved in the decision-making process and communicates as much information as possible throughout a project.

Strengths

- Committed and detail-oriented
- Accomplished with a meticulous nature.
- Empathetic and understanding.

Weaknesses

- Defensive and guarded
- Demanding and opinionated.
- Loyal to the point of being oblivious to others' needs.

Best career choices: Therapy and counseling, human resources, baking, psychology, nursing, nutrition, hospitality, medicine, catering, real estate, anthropology, archeology, teaching, and social work.

Worst career choices: You're very emotional, so you will likely not do well with any job requiring practicality. Stay away from marketing because you are not a person who likes to take risks. Also, stay away from politics, insurance, and stock trading.

Leo at Work

Leos seek recognition and appreciation, even when they are in the workplace. They are known for their good looks and confidence, making them great leaders and potential influencers. However, this is also a sign prone to being overly dramatic at times. So, when things don't go as intended, Leos have a hard time not taking it personally.

If you are working with someone who is a Leo, make sure you take a moment before responding to their comments or criticism. Sometimes, Leos will be too self-centered in their decisions, causing others to feel they are not involved in matters concerning them.

A Leo sun sign's presence can seem larger than life, which is beneficial for those around them. But it can also be a challenge to maintain diplomatic relationships with other people due to Leos' tendency toward being overbearing and arrogant. If you're a Leo, it is important to remind yourself that others may not be as pleased with how well you are doing as you are. It could cause your colleagues to question whether they are truly committed to the project and believe in how hard they worked on a particular project.

Leo people are temperamental and competitive, making them successful at work, but they need help learning to work more collaboratively with their co-workers.

Strengths
- Witty and charming
- Intelligent and ambitious
- Innovative and forward-thinking.

Weaknesses
- Volatile and unpredictable
- Dictatorial and overbearing
- Resentful of others' success.

Best career choices: Politics, ambassadorship, acting, modeling, fashion, diplomacy, entrepreneurship, event managing, media strategy. You can also be a spokesperson, civil servant, minister, or chief executive.

Worst career choices: You don't do well with authority and taking orders, so stay away from backend jobs. Also, avoid work where you can't interact with the public.

Virgo at Work

The Virgo sun sign is organized and efficient. They are ideal employees but can also cause others to mistake Virgo's efficiency for stubbornness. Virgo people are deeply analytical, which means they will frequently question every decision or action, making it difficult to interact with their colleagues.

It takes a lot of hard work to make it in the workplace, and Virgos often have more than their fair share. Moreover, this sign struggles to get along with others because they struggle with criticism. This can create friction in a team since only one person can get their point across. Virgos must learn how to effectively communicate when they feel frustrated or neglected by the lack of recognition for their hard work.

Remember, your co-workers are humans too and are only doing what they think is best for the organization. So, work out your differences by approaching your colleagues respectfully.

Strengths

- Methodical and detail-oriented
- Thorough and attentive to details.
- Efficient and practical.

Weaknesses

- Impractical and pessimistic.
- Critical of others' work.
- Resentful of the praise others receive for their work.
- Overly analytical to the point of being inflexible or indecisive.

Best career choices: Investigation, translation, editing, designing, detective work, statistician, hospitality, nutrition, veterinary medicine, quantity surveying, auditing, accounting.

Worst career choices: You won't be successful working in security or any job involving adventure.

Libra at Work

The Libra sun sign is diplomatic, which can be a good trait in the workplace. However, this sign struggles with decision-making, taking on responsibility, and being assertive. It makes them appear wishy-washy to their colleagues because they try so hard to be liked by everyone.

Ensure that your Libra co-worker understands the demands of their position within the company and the importance of reaching deadlines. Allow them to provide input on a project before starting so that they are engaged and committed. They will feel that their ideas and needs are considered before taking any action.

Watch for signs of frustration or disappointment in your co-worker. This could indicate they are uncomfortable with the amount of responsibility placed on their shoulders, which should be discussed to avoid future issues.

Libra people are also indecisive and uncomfortable discussing new ideas or difficult decision-making. Typically, Libra is happy to work as part of a team since they appreciate other opinions and viewpoints for decision-making.

Strengths

- Diplomatic
- Able to juggle different responsibilities
- Sensitive to others' needs

Weaknesses

- Impractical
- Wishy-washy and indecisive
- Malleable and lacking in commitment or focus
- Easily disconnected from project goals or timelines
- Unrealistic regarding deadlines, budgets, or expectations for the project

Best career choices: Law, negotiation, detective work, human resources, counseling, styling, interior design, diplomacy, negotiation, mediation, event planning, lobbying.

Worst career choices: Stay away from jobs that require you to make critical decisions on the go.

Scorpio at Work

The Scorpio sun sign is passionate, imaginative, and highly intuitive. They can analyze data and make quick decisions easily since they can look at situations from multiple angles.

Scorpios often have difficulty asking for help since they believe that seeking assistance makes them seem weak. This causes them to struggle with delegation since they are afraid of how others will react if they can't handle everything themselves.

Scorpios are usually overly critical and hurt or upset others because of the way they interact with the Scorpio in the workplace.

Scorpios must remember their co-workers are also human, even if they don't agree with their opinions or actions. Listen to your co-workers and remember they only want to help you.

Strengths

- Brilliant and inventive
- Dedicated and passionate
- Likable
- Intuitive and insightful

Weaknesses

- Possessive of their territory or achievements.
- Overly dramatic or moody
- Quick to anger or resentment.
- Ruthless when dealing with competition or threats to their success.

Best career choices: Engineering, spy work, surgery, science, research, engineering, fertility matters, market analysis, business analysis, occultism, secret service, psychology, financial advising, astrology.

Worst career choices: Stay away from jobs without any deeper meaning. For instance, translation, cooking, statistics, and mathematics.

Sagittarius at Work

The Sagittarius sun sign is enthusiastic and optimistic, making them great colleagues since their sense of humor lightens the mood in tense situations. However, they are open-minded, making them seem flaky or disorganized in the workplace.

Sagittarius people need to learn to be more organized and focused at work to use their time more efficiently and get the recognition and advancement they seek.

Sagittarius is also drawn to the opposite sex, so it could be difficult for them to concentrate on their work in the office with their colleagues. Sagittarius people must learn to resist temptation and concentrate on their careers. It will allow them to make great connections at work and foster relationships to help them in the future.

Strengths

- Ambitious
- Persistent and tenacious.
- Adventurous and daring.
- Creative and lively.

Weaknesses

- Naive and erratic.
- Irrational and impractical.
- Impractical, inconsistent, or unreliable.
- Wishful thinkers or overly optimistic.

Best career choices: Travel sales, public relations, administration, entertainment, recreation, adventure, tourism, theology, life coaching, politics, public speaking, piloting, sports, spirituality, entrepreneurship, detective work.

Worst career choices: Stay away from everything mundane. Also, you don't do well working where your efforts aren't recognized, or you're shackled to a chair, like a ghostwriter, copy editor, or any other desk job.

Capricorn at Work

Capricorns are pragmatic and disciplined, making them a great fit for the workplace. However, they are also overly analytical and critical of others, which makes it difficult for them to relate to others in the office since they seem cold or distant.

Capricorns must avoid being critical of their colleagues or appearing aloof or uninterested in others. Instead, they should recognize that this is their natural tendency when under stress and learn to deal with it so that it does not affect their effectiveness in the office.

This sign is serious, disciplined, and efficient in whatever they do, making them ideal employees and great leaders. They are very goal-oriented and can also motivate others to succeed. However, watch for signs of frustration from your Capricorn co-worker since they bottle up their feelings rather than address them. Capricorn people must be given feedback on their performance regularly. This allows them to reflect on where they can improve.

Also, give your Capricorn co-worker any praise and recognition they deserve, especially in a public forum where it will be noticed by everyone else, too.

Strengths
- Efficient and effective
- Disciplined and organized
- Entrepreneurial and innovative.

Weaknesses
- Unemotional or cold.
- Controlled or aloof.
- Reserved or indifferent.
- Lacks focus or follow-through.

• May intimidate others with their cool demeanor.

Best career choices: Banking, law, information technology, medicine, science, accounting, administration, business execution, physics, financial planning, business, consultancy, logistics, science, and supply chain management. You can also be a physics scholar or a CEO.

Worst career choices: There is nothing you love more than financial excellence, so you must take a job where you are adequately compensated. Stay away from all jobs requiring adventure or having to make decisions in the heat of the moment.

Aquarius at Work

Aquarius is hardworking and determined. They are also open-minded and accept differing opinions, making them a great asset to the office environment. However, they struggle with accepting criticism, so it's essential to give them feedback so they can evaluate their work performance.

Aquarius people are too emotional in the workplace, which can cause them to act carelessly or fall prey to their emotions when dealing with co-workers. They cannot focus on one particular thing all day long as other signs do. It causes difficulties for them in their career and prevents them from meeting their goals.

The Aquarius sun sign is quite independent and unconventional, making it difficult for Aquarius people to work with their colleagues since they often don't fit into the company culture.

It is important to watch for signs of dissatisfaction from your Aquarius co-worker since they could be struggling with isolation or rejection. It is hard for them to talk about their problems if they are afraid you'll think they are just complaining about everything. As an Aquarius, if you feel something does not seem right, it is best to speak up about the situation rather than wait until something negative happens before you can intervene.

Strengths

• Innovative and original

• Independent and dedicated

• Persistent and tenacious

Weaknesses

- Overly critical or cynical.
- Prone to depression.
- Unstable and changeable.
- Aloof, distant, or uninterested in other people's lives.
- Suspicious, paranoid, or untrusting of others.

Best career choices: Music, invention, exploration, science, concept-building, computer development, electronics, photography, communication, astrology, agriculture, aeronautics, environmental activism, and market research.

Worst career choices: It is not for you if your job does not allow you to use your innovative gift. Stay away from the conventional, and do not attempt to become an officer of the law.

Pisces at Work

Pisces people are moody and fickle, so it is difficult to concentrate in the workplace. They do not have the focus required to succeed in a job setting. They will become overwhelmed and distracted by everything around them.

Pisces people often have trouble communicating their emotions, and they seem distant and cold in the workplace. Pisces people must learn to express their feelings more often to be taken more seriously.

The Pisces sun sign is very sensitive and intuitive. You are difficult to offend, but you can be easily overwhelmed by the emotions of others.

Pisces people need to learn to take things less personally and focus on the bigger picture instead of getting bogged down with animosity or jealousy from their co-workers. Be sure that your Pisces co-worker understands their role in the company and what is expected of them before starting any new projects or tasks.

Strengths

- Warm and compassionate
- Highly intuitive
- Great team player.

Weaknesses

- Torn between the demands of personal life and work.
- Can be a victim of mistreatment.
- Subject to being emotionally manipulated by others or giving in to peer pressure.

Best career choices: You can be an artist, animator, social worker, philanthropist, psychic therapist, recruiter, hairstylist, nurse, theme park designer, psychologist, physiotherapist, or teacher.

Worst career choices: Financial gain isn't so important because you're not practical. You don't care much for jobs that are restrictive with your time. Do not attempt to join the armed forces or become a stock trader or banker.

Chapter 5: Zodiac Houses and Their Meanings

The zodiac is split into twelve parts known as houses. Each house is led by one sign and connected to very specific qualities, starting with your personality and extending outward to society and the universe. Every celestial body is in set houses and signs when you're born. So, interpreting your natal chart involves factoring in the influence of each planet, noting their houses and the signs, to help you determine your hidden gifts and future struggles in this incarnation.

When a planet is in a house, it imbues that house with its energies and inevitably affects your life. This is how an astrologer knows which aspects of life need attention at a particular point and how you can effectively deal with the things that happen to you. Houses one through six are personal houses, while houses seven through twelve are interpersonal houses.

The Houses

The first house is the house of all things "first." It's about fresh beginnings, the self, and how you look. It's about first impressions, your body, and how you identify in life. It's the way you deal with things in life. Aries governs this house.

The second house: This house deals with your physical surroundings and senses. It is associated with your line of work, how you attract finances, your values, the things that matter most to you, and your habits. It's ruled by Taurus.

The third house: This house governs how you communicate and think. It's about your interests, your education, and your neighbors. It's about schools, teachers, and travel in your immediate environment and community. Gemini governs it.

The fourth house: Ruled by Cancer, it's the house of home. It's all about foundations, connected to your roots, how you care for yourself, your emotions, children, motherhood, and everything pertaining to a woman.

The fifth house: This is Leo's turf. It's about your love affairs and romantic life. It's also in charge of the way you express yourself, childlike exuberance, play, creativity, joy, and the drama in your life.

The sixth house: It's Virgo's territory. It's about the organization, work ethic, systems, fitness, general health, and the desire to be useful and service to everyone.

The seventh house: Libra's house is about your connections to others in relationships, business, marriage, and contracts. It's about how you relate and share with other people.

The eighth house: This house concerns merging with others, intimacy, mystery, and sex. It's also in charge of your property, assets, loans, inheritances, and how you share finances and resources with your partner. It is Scorpio's house.

The ninth house: This house is in charge of travel, discovery, learning, philosophy, wisdom, religion, and law. Sagittarius rules it, so it's about relating to people from different cultures.

The tenth house: Capricorn reigns here. This house is about your career, expertise, long-term goals, public perception, status, and reputation. It's also connected to masculinity and fatherhood.

The eleventh house: Governed by Aquarius, this house is in charge of connection to groups, friendships, and your society's awareness. It's also about your future dreams and hopes, your eccentric side, and how you deal with sudden changes.

The twelfth house: This is the house of endings. It's all about wrapping things up, the afterlife, getting old, and surrendering. It's a house that also involves separating yourself from the rest of the world, hidden plans, hospitals, imprisonment, and other institutions. Ruled by Pisces, it's also in charge of your subconscious mind, the arts, and imagination.

Now that you know what all the houses are about, let's look at each zodiac sign in each house and how it's likely to affect you.

The Signs in Each House

Aries

Aries is the first house: You have a highly developed sense of individuality and self-awareness. You don't like being told what to do but prefer being in charge of your life. Your personality is open to new ideas and opportunities, so you're always searching for something that makes you feel more alive or brings a spark back into your life.

Aries in the second house: The people in your friendship circle may not consider you very social. You have strong desires and interests but prefer a private life. You may get along well with your cousins, who share some personality traits.

Aries in the third house: Some time ago, you may have gone through a very difficult personal situation that caused you to change your life. Thankfully, you overcame this obstacle and learned an important lesson about common sense and staying connected to other people. Being separated from people makes you lonely and depressed.

Aries in the fourth house: You have a great memory and excellent sense of direction. There's a place inside you that you might keep hidden from most people. It's your inner place, perhaps your retreat or sanctuary. Only you have access to this hidden place, where you go to take a break from the rest of the world and recharge your batteries.

Aries in the fifth house: The main lesson you've learned since coming into this world is that it's healthy and necessary to enjoy life fully. You want to live with more spontaneity and fewer restrictions from other people to express yourself more freely. This lesson may be difficult for you to learn, so you do something silly in an attempt to make a point.

Aries in the sixth house: Your environment, especially your neighborhood, has a tremendous impact on your personality. You have an inherent sense of security and well-being when surrounded by people you know and who like being with you. You feel so comfortable that it's hard to imagine stepping outside those boundaries.

Aries in the seventh house: A unique quality about your life expresses itself through money made and used daily. You are prone to saving money in anticipation of an unexpected event, like an illness or a new car. You probably believe that keeping a certain amount of money aside is more important than spending it.

Aries in the eighth house: Your home is your primary source of security, comfort, and love. It represents stability and security, so you're very protective of it. Although you may find yourself frustrated with a situation related to your home, you take comfort that it's always there whenever things get rough, or life gets too difficult to handle.

Aries in the ninth house: Your mind is always filled with ideas and thoughts. You like to keep busy, so it's important to organize your time to allow you to do what you truly enjoy. Many things interest and spark your imagination, but you get bored and lose interest quickly once you get started on something.

Aries in the tenth house: You naturally take charge of things. When others start panicking, or the situation seems too difficult, you jump in and take command of the situation. This is beneficial in many ways, but you have to be careful not to let it go too far. You don't want to get so involved that you become a dictator, especially if you're in a leadership position.

Aries in the eleventh house: You define your personality and vitality by the friends surrounding you and the activities you participate in together. You may get emotionally involved with people and like or dislike them based on silly things they say or do. This creates problems since other people react in kind, creating tension between you.

Aries in the twelfth house: Your spiritual growth is directly connected to your mental state. You become obsessed with things that don't matter or want to convert people when it's inappropriate. Your efforts in this area often come from your core beliefs or religion, so you're coming from a place of strength.

Taurus

Taurus is the first house: You have a great ability to attract people with your sense of security and stability, but this is not always the best thing for you. You have an inner strength that's always there, even when things look bad on the surface. You know how to relax and enjoy life, so you're usually surrounded by good friends you love.

Taurus is the second house: You know how to get what you want. Money is important, but not for the usual reasons. You're not interested in being rich but rather having enough money to do what you want to do. You have a very practical approach to life, but it's often wiser than it first appears to be.

Taurus in the third house: You're very stable, and people depend on you for advice or a place to stay when they're in a bad situation. Your powers of concentration are almost superhuman, and you're an expert at focusing on one thing at a time. Nothing will distract you when your mind is focused with laser-like intensity on something until it's done.

Taurus in the fourth house: Your home will likely be a very solid, comfortable, and secure place. You're sensitive to your family members and therefore make a great parent. Many family members turn to you for help with their problems, so you need to learn when to say no.

Taurus in the fifth house: You are a sensualist and love physical pleasures like food, drink, sex, and touch. Your love life is always important, but it's best if you don't make it too complicated, or jealous situations may be the result. Your ability to look at things sensibly will help keep jealousy at bay.

Taurus in the sixth house: You are very attentive to your home and will do everything to keep it feeling comfortable and attractive. Your sense of aesthetics is strong, and you use it to ensure the place looks pleasing.

Taurus in the seventh house: You approach things practically, but there's always an artistic streak that makes you want to sit down with a pen and paper and create. You express yourself best through music, painting, or writing because these are ways you communicate your feelings, which sometimes go unspoken between friends.

Taurus in the eighth house: Money isn't as important, but you are tempted to take advantage of someone else's finances sometimes in your life. Protect your money from others, and don't let anyone borrow from you.

Taurus in the ninth house: You have a strong sense of justice and see things as black or white. Most people think of this as a spiritual house and feel drawn toward religion, philosophy, or metaphysics. You're very patient with people and love showing them new experiences.

Taurus in the tenth house: You have a lot of drive and organizational ability needed for success in your career. You're willing to work hard for what you want and will achieve it in time.

Taurus in the eleventh house: Friends are very important, and you do anything to help them if needed. Your friends find you very dependable and responsible, but at times they also find you a bit stubborn, even lazy, because you're more comfortable than ambitious.

Taurus in the twelfth house: You're very good at concealing the things you want to hide. People can't tell what you want to hide, but you know. Your love of secrets makes you vulnerable and insecure, so don't let anyone see the real person behind them, or they could hurt you.

Gemini

Gemini in the first house: You are a very intelligent and quick-witted person. You often have many ideas simultaneously, but you can't put them into action all at once. So, it is hard for you to get things done, and sometimes you find yourself not doing what you want to do. You need a structure for things to move forward.

Gemini in the second house: You take a lot of risks with what you do and say, mostly because your mind is constantly moving incredibly fast. Often, people don't always understand you, so they think your unpredictability will cause problems sooner or later. When decision-making, keep this in mind because it won't always work out as expected.

Gemini is the third house: You are a very curious person and never let anything stand in the way of true knowledge. You find it very hard to make decisions, especially financially. It is easy to lose your money by spending frivolously or wasting time on unimportant things.

Gemini in the fourth house: You have many friends who know what is best for them because of your levelheadedness. However, they soon become interested in other things that have nothing to do with you, and your thoughts get lost in the shuffle. You need to know when to stop and focus on yourself.

Gemini in the fifth house: You are an optimistic person always looking for the good in things. You may not be as practical as other people, but you are always open and honest. You love learning new things and having a good time, but this doesn't mean that you don't work hard during the day.

Gemini in the sixth house: You love to travel, even if this means leaving your home for vacations or business trips. Your mind is very active, so it is easy to get distracted, so traveling keeps you very busy and stimulated.

Gemini in the seventh house: You are a very social person and love to be with people. Your love for human interaction is hard to resist, but this makes it hard to stay focused on one thing at a time. You always want to keep your mind busy, and sometimes it conflicts with other people who want to work alone.

Gemini in the eighth house: Even though you are a very intelligent person, you don't always make the wisest decisions with your finances. You like putting yourself into situations that make your heart race or cause you stress. For example, you often spend more money than you should and then feel bad about it.

Gemini in the ninth house: You are a very curious individual who loves learning new things and can learn from other people's experiences. You are also very easy to get along with, making it easy for friends to trust you with their lives. It makes you a very reliable person and causes others to hold back information too important to reveal.

Gemini in the tenth house: You have a lot of ideas that surface from your subconscious mind, and these ideas are hard for people to understand at times. It isn't easy to get your ideas and plans approved by others. If you want to succeed, you need to learn to explain yourself for people to get your message.

Gemini in the eleventh house: You are the life of the party and don't mind going out at night to a place filled with people. You love being around people who have new information or new thoughts, but sometimes this is overwhelming when you have to focus on a single thing.

Gemini in the twelfth house: You have a very active imagination when awake and when dreaming. It is difficult to make decisions, especially when it negatively affects your life's direction. You need to learn how to overcome this by talking about your thoughts and plans.

Cancer

Cancer in the first house: You are an emotional and sensitive person who holds everything in. You want to express yourself but find it hard to put your thoughts into words. This is also true when you want to remember things; they often seem vague or foggy.

Cancer is the second house: You are a very generous person, and you like buying people presents or giving them money because of how they make you feel. You can earn a lot of money because you are smart and hard-working. However, this could cause financial problems because you spend more than you earn. You also find it difficult to save your money for future goals or emergencies, but this can be overcome with discipline and organization skills.

Cancer in the third house: You love to communicate and express your thoughts very easily, and you enjoy writing letters and reading novels. You are intelligent and have a great memory, but you struggle to concentrate on important things or constructive work.

Cancer is the fourth house: This position gives you a great appreciation for home comforts and security. You love having your own space, so your surroundings must make you feel comfortable. You worry about security and safety, even though you are a careful person.

Cancer in the fifth house: You have a very strong sense of justice and fairness, especially with money issues. You like to judge people, which makes you very intolerant of others, often leading to a bad temper. Crime and legal issues usually interest you.

Cancer in the sixth house: This position reveals many facets of yourself and makes it hard to put yourself into one category or type. You have an emotional mind that goes from anger one minute to happiness the next. You also have difficulty getting along with co-workers, often causing you much stress.

Cancer in the seventh house: This position makes you want to get married and have a family, even though you're very shy around people. You are loving but also very moody. You make friends easily, but sometimes this leads to jealousy from friends or rivals. You like spending time with your partner or spouse, and you want them to be happy above all else.

Cancer in the eighth house: You have a strong sense of material wealth and assets you need to protect. These are very important because they represent security and safety. Even though you are a careful person, you enjoy spending a lot of money on unnecessary gadgets and objects.

Cancer in the ninth house: This position makes you very happy and energetic, but it also causes your moodiness to worsen. You have strong personal beliefs and morals that guide your life, and you worry about your health because you're anxious about it being too good or too bad. You will likely get involved in political issues since this is where you feel the most energy and get the most pleasure.

Cancer in the tenth house: This position gives you an analytical mind that is critical of other people at times, so you struggle to communicate with others. You are a very sociable person and love to spend time with others, but if someone is not being friendly or civil, it will make you very angry.

Cancer in the eleventh house: This position makes you good at decision-making, and you can clearly see what needs to be done. You are very logical and have no emotions, so you don't always experience true happiness in your life or with others around you. Often, you make enemies because people cannot understand you or the logic in your decisions.

Cancer in the twelfth house: This position gives emotional intelligence that causes your moodiness to worsen. You will likely get involved in legal issues because of your passion for making the wrongs right in your head. You prefer privacy and ensuring that your emotions are in control around other people, even though they may be very difficult to hide.

Leo

Leo in the first house: You are very much a leader and highly ambitious. You want to be the best in everything, which could cause many challenges. Even though people like being around you because of your warmth and goodwill, others dislike you for your direct personality.

Leo in the second house: You struggle with financial problems because of your lack of organizational skills or money discipline. You love spending money on luxurious items, causing financial problems because you keep spending more than is sensible. There is also a good chance that you'll be involved in a scandal.

Leo in the third house: You are very popular, and people like being around you because of your warmth and goodwill. You are extremely loyal to people who have been kind to you, as long as they treat you well, making it easy for the wrong people to get close to you.

Leo in the fourth house: People have a problem with your leadership ability or views on life, especially if those views are contrary to what everyone else thinks and does. This possibly causes a great deal of difficulty when making friends because people will avoid you for being too forceful about your beliefs.

Leo in the fifth house: This is a lucky placement, as Leo rules the fifth house. In love, these people shine, and they love with all of their hearts. They approach love with a carefree heart just like a child would. Creativity flows out of these individuals; they don't have a shortage of ideas. These natives know how to truly enjoy the pleasures of life.

Libra

Libra is the first house: You go overboard with your hobbies or interests, which often causes social embarrassments. Exercise self-control before spending your hard-earned money on things that only bring you negative attention.

Libra is the second house: You love having things around you that make you feel especially good, like beautiful artwork or expensive jewelry. It's essential not to be addicted to these things and limit your spending because you'll eventually run out of money for necessities.

Libra is the third house: You put others down in their appearance, which is not very attractive when people look at a romantic relationship between you and another person. Be more humble; you'll get further in life.

Libra is the fourth house: You push things away and keep them a secret. Maybe it is because of your resentment toward your parents or their values, or maybe you are hiding something from yourself. Whatever the case, don't bottle up your true feelings.

Libra in the fifth house: You have a lot of fun with others and make life exciting whenever you hang out. Remember, other people might not be as outgoing as you, so don't judge them.

Libra in the sixth house: You value beauty and harmony, which is good for your work ethic and how you handle yourself in the workplace. However, don't get too caught up with the aesthetic of your workspace, and focus more on finding a balance between beauty and productivity.

Libra in the seventh house: You want others to be happy and make them feel beautiful, which is great. Just don't forget about yourself when you're doing things for others because you also deserve happiness. If someone doesn't appreciate you for who you are, they aren't worth your time.

Libra in the eighth house: You are very judgmental towards others, even when those you judge are your friends. Be more understanding and not so quick to judge people behind their backs.

Libra in the ninth house: You have a fondness for beauty and harmony that causes you to make rash decisions or give in to your desires without thinking them through. Sometimes it's better to say no rather than yes.

Libra in the tenth house: You can easily get overwhelmed by everything that needs fixing around your home or workplace; you shouldn't impose yourself on these issues immediately if they don't need you. Instead, focus your energy on things you can control or are good at doing.

Libra in the eleventh house: You are self-conscious when around others and take criticism personally. It's better for people to be honest with you about their feelings than to hide them from you.

Libra in the twelfth house: Your artistic abilities will likely get overlooked because you feel you must blend in with others. Don't be afraid of expressing yourself, even if it means being a little eccentric now and then.

Scorpio

Scorpio in the first house: You want to use your attention to attract people in your life and to know how beautiful you think they are. However, it may be difficult for others to see that beauty because of how you treat them. Be a little more patient.

Scorpio is the second house: Your energy is overwhelming and intimidating when socializing, so hold back on your energy when meeting new people.

Scorpio is the third house: Your mind is always on the go, and you are always contemplating how to make people fall in love with you. However, your best bet is to tell them who and what you are so they can make their own conclusions. Be a little more authentic.

Scorpio in the fourth house: Your energy is sometimes hard for people to handle because you are deeply spiritual, mysterious, and intense. Fortunately, this doesn't bother you much because you don't care what anybody thinks about you anyway. The problem is that it doesn't work with your interests and passions.

Scorpio in the fifth house: You are deeply charismatic and quite magnetic to others. Your attention is a bit more of a burden than it would seem, so be less intense with people. There is nothing wrong with being attentive, but sometimes it overwhelms others.

Scorpio in the sixth house: You care about how you treat other people around you, so it might come off as controlling. Let go of your emotions and admit when something bothers you. People won't have to guess what is on your mind.

Scorpio in the seventh house: Intimidating and mysterious, you give people a hard time by the way you present yourself. The only way you'll enjoy a good relationship is if you are more open. You have nothing to worry about.

Scorpio in the eighth house: Your intensity can be too much for some people to handle, but that doesn't stop you from being who you want to be. Your intense energy is very intimidating, but people are drawn to it anyway because it is you they are attracted to.

Scorpio in the ninth house: Your intensity isn't easy for people to handle because you want to control everything. You need to lighten up and realize your intensity is probably one of your biggest strengths. However, don't push it on others.

Scorpio in the tenth house: You have a lot of potential for your future goals because of your intensity and focus. You will further reach those goals if you are more flexible with people and don't push so hard.

Scorpio in the eleventh house: You are intensely passionate about everything you do, which is positive. However, your intensity may be a bit much for some people, so be more subtle with your passion and intense energy.

Scorpio in the twelfth house: You're intensely focused on what you want out of life. You are drawn to deep mysteries and life secrets because of who your energy attracts. It's good to have those interests but focus less on them for stronger relationships with people.

Sagittarius

Sagittarius in the first house: You are a bit of an adventurer, and being around new people and exploring your surroundings. However, your adventurous nature can get in the way of making friends.

Sagittarius in the second house: You aren't afraid to be notified for socializing and meeting new people, but people may not know what you want from a relationship. Spend more time alone with your thoughts before looking for a person who will match them.

Sagittarius is the third house: You are free-spirited and spontaneous around others. You have a positive attitude toward life and don't mind joking around. You're an extrovert who loves to talk.

Sagittarius in the fourth house: You may have difficulty making your downtime feel like something much more important than relaxing. However, be careful not to let your imagination run wild and consume all your energy. Make sure you stay active to release that extra energy and not feel guilty about being inactive for a while each day.

Sagittarius in the fifth house: You have a good ability to see the bigger picture and are not afraid to explore people who aren't as well-liked. You are a people-pleaser and want to please everyone around you. You cannot get stuck on making your friends happy all of the time as it will cause problems making new friends or developing new interests.

Sagittarius in the sixth house: You have a good ability to connect with others, making it easier for you to build relationships. However, your fondness for being around people may lead you to do counterproductive things when you find someone special. Don't feel pressured to have a connection when you meet someone. Rather open yourself to the world and new things instead of building connections familiar to you.

Sagittarius in the seventh house: You may feel like people do not trust you, but it's better to stay than change how others see you. This sign is at its most relaxed before making a long-term commitment in a relationship. You may not feel comfortable in the spotlight, but you must let people see your bright side so they see your potential for success in life.

Sagittarius in the eighth house: You are prone to committing yourself to projects you feel responsible for, but don't let this stop you from reaching your full potential. You're a person eager to take what you are doing and finish it yourself, and that's fine, but don't lock yourself in your room. Release your energy, so it helps you focus and make new friends.

Sagittarius in the ninth house: You love experiencing new things and being around people who enjoy adventuring as much as you. However, you are prone to taking too many risks in things that interest you. You often feel like you've already experienced life at its best. Take a step back and see what else life has to offer.

Sagittarius in the tenth house: You're a romantic and always looking for someone special that will make you feel they are worth your time and attention. However, you are often unsure how you feel about people in your life. Spend more time with people you don't consider your ultimate match until you determine how interested you are in them.

Sagittarius in the eleventh house: You look at things differently and see things others do not. You have a great memory, so it's hard to forget the past, especially in relationships.

Sagittarius in the twelfth house: You like experimenting, but this excitement for life can be difficult to control. Whatever you are interested in, be careful not to go off the deep end. Be more open-minded about new experiences and people.

Capricorn

Capricorn is the first house: You have a sharp mind and are always looking for ways to make quick money. You also don't mind putting in some extra work to get what you want and will probably start working at a young age.

Capricorn in the second house: You likely spend time understanding how the world works and how to invest your funds. You've probably learned to save money from an early age.

Capricorn is the third house: You like being around people but are prone to shyness and feel too much pressure when first getting involved with others. However, don't think about why people aren't talking to you.

Capricorn in the fourth house: You have been the child to get chores done early, which means you have a good understanding of managing your money. You value security and like things to be in order. Sometimes it is difficult to tell others what's wrong or how you feel.

Capricorn in the fifth house: As a child, you probably found it easy to concentrate on your studies or hobbies for an extended period and preferred not to have been disturbed. You are tidy and organized, so living in a mess is an uncomfortable experience.

Capricorn in the sixth house: You are ambitious and disciplined but find it difficult to make time for yourself. You are serious in everything you do, so sometimes you come across as cold and uninterested.

Capricorn in the seventh house: You were likely the one child with few friends due to your shyness or awkwardness around others, or you were more interested in things other than people.

Capricorn in the eighth house: You may have grown up a little more timid and reserved than other children and had less-than-welcoming relationships. You like to control your surroundings and are likely to be established early in life.

Capricorn in the ninth house: As a child, you preferred not to participate in fun or exciting things. You probably even went as far as to avoid any opportunity for fun, lest you were left with no choice but to join in.

Capricorn in the tenth house: You had few friends growing up, as you were more interested in being serious than people. You most likely wanted to be grown-up early in life and preferred responsibilities over playtime.

Capricorn in the eleventh house: Your childhood could have been insecure or difficult, as you never felt completely secure regarding your place in the world. You may have been teased or disliked by others for merely being who you are.

Capricorn in the twelfth house: You are very responsible and reliable and don't need much encouragement to get started on anything. You grew up feeling like you didn't fit in and were probably teased for being different.

Aquarius

Aquarius in the first house: People tend to think of you as a fun-loving and positive person who doesn't let anything get them down. You probably spent time with others your age and were quite the social butterfly as a child.

Aquarius in the second house: You are a frugal person and don't mind hard work to buy what you want. The first things you bought were probably practical or would last a long time.

Aquarius in the third house: You are something of an oddball, as even from an early age, you had different interests from others. It probably started with your first love, whatever that was. This brought about your social awkwardness among others as you portray yourself differently.

Aquarius in the fourth house: There's nothing better than indulging your curiosity by learning more about people and their quirks. It leads to meeting like-minded people and forming strong bonds.

Aquarius in the fifth house: You are someone who isn't afraid to stand up for what you believe in and make it known across town. It can result in heated debates and also a lot of admiration from people who appreciate your determination.

Aquarius in the sixth house: People may consider you a health freak due to your obsession with staying healthy. You'll likely go above and beyond what is required to keep yourself or those around you healthy.

Aquarius in the seventh house: You're a unique person when it comes to love. You often fall for unpopular people much different from yourself and even with opposing points of view. This causes disputes between friends and other loved ones, but they don't last long because of your strong bond.

Aquarius in the eighth house: You are a very generous person, always willing to help those in need, even if you don't know them personally. The only problem with this is that when you need help, people are not willing to repay the favor.

Aquarius in the ninth house: You are one of the most interesting individuals and never cease to surprise those around you. Your determination to solve problems and discover what makes things tick makes interesting conversations with others. Your impulsive nature will lead others astray if they follow your example.

Aquarius in the tenth house: You are someone with a strong sense of spirituality and morality. Although you can be eccentric, you do not choose to act this way on purpose. Instead, it is because you can't help but think things through to their conclusion.

Aquarius in the eleventh house: You have a very well-developed intuitive nature between people and yourself. You struggle to believe if things about others are true or not, but you'll find out soon enough through what people say about you in public.

Aquarius in the twelfth house: You are a very realistic person having little trouble living and dealing with the realities of life. Your intuition is very strong, and you can easily tell if you're being lied to or if a person is truly trying to help you. You can usually differentiate between what's important and what's not.

Pisces

Pisces is the first house: You have a very strong personality, which sometimes makes it difficult for people to relate to you because you are so stubborn. You have a hard time being wrong, and it is often impossible to admit that you are.

Pisces in the second house: Due to your dreamy nature as a child, many of your early interests and hobbies revolved around fantasy and not reality. It doesn't mean you didn't learn to do things in real life, but instead, you struggle to comprehend something until you see it.

Pisces in the third house: You are highly creative and imaginative. When you get an idea, you have to act on it. You also have a very high pain tolerance and are very good at finding ways to make things work or take care of things that go wrong.

Pisces in the fourth house: You have a great love for entertainment, so you have a hard time with real-life responsibilities and problems because your mind needs something more interesting than reality to occupy itself.

Pisces in the fifth house: You have problems in romance and relationships because you are too idealistic with unrealistic expectations.

Pisces in the sixth house: You struggle with authority due to your larger-than-life imagination, which puts you in the positions of authority figures, and then you rebel against them.

Pisces in the seventh house: You have difficulty with marriage and partnerships, whether business or personal. You battle to confide in people, and people find it hard to confide in you, resulting in a lack of communication between partners.

Pisces in the eighth house: You are very mercenary-like with your money and possessions. However, this quality is not for self-gain but rather for the benefit of others.

Pisces in the ninth house: You have a great deal of trouble believing in religion. You cannot comprehend something that can't be proven or isn't entirely concrete.

Pisces in the tenth house: Settling down or even committing to your job is a struggle because it is too hard to focus on one thing for extended periods. Your mind just keeps wandering, making you restless and desiring to be somewhere else.

Pisces in the eleventh house: You have a very hard time with friends due to your extreme sensitivity. This sensitivity makes it difficult to form relationships because you are too quick to take things other people say about you personally.

Pisces in the twelfth house: Discovering anything about yourself is extremely difficult because it requires self-awareness, which is rare in Pisces. However, when you learn something about yourself, it can be extremely profound and affect every aspect of your life.

Chapter 6: Planetary Placements

Planetary placements are precisely what they sound like. It refers to where the planets are positioned during your birth or at any point in time, like an important event in history or in your life. These placements are why we can get information about our lives through astrology, what determines our character, and why two people with the same sun signs can be very different. Let's get into the various planet positions in each of the twelve houses without further ado.

The Planets in Each House

Sun

Sun in the first house: You're a very active person, a person to start new things and who takes pride in what you've accomplished. You have a personality that shines, and when needed, you can be assertive with grace and dignity. You're a natural leader and a pretty successful one at that.

Sun in the second house: The spotlight shines especially bright for you. You're self-assured, strong, and capable of great things. You have the drive to excel, and this translates into your career.

Sun in the third house: This is the house of your appearance, social standing, and good judgment. You're observant and have a knack for quick decision-making based on what you observe first thing in the morning.

Sun in the fourth house: Your home is your haven, where you shed yourself of troubles by submerging yourself in family life. Your home will represent everything that makes you happy or feel safe and at peace. You place romance high on your priority list.

Sun in the fifth house: You're sociable and fun to be around. It's easy for you to make friends because of your approachable demeanor, and it's equally as easy for you to get along with people at work. You love yourself, but you also love helping others.

Sun in the sixth house: As your home is your haven, this is also where you go when you want to retreat from all the hustle and bustle of city life. It's a place of solitude that allows you time to think things through carefully and rationally.

Sun in the seventh house: Successful relationships await your notice. Something worth noting here is that the relationship you have with your spouse, partner, or life partner will be very important. So, pay more attention to this aspect of life, especially a long-term committed relationship.

Sun in the eighth house: You draw strength from your family and friends. Your home is also a place of comfort and serenity, and that's the way you like it. You're very close to the money, as you're fiscally responsible.

Sun in the ninth house: It's time to change scenery. You seek out freedom from all your problems, particularly from the rigors of city life. This is where you should take some time off to travel for fun and relaxation, or sometimes just for enjoyment's sake.

Sun in the tenth house: You have a lot to offer others through your expertise and experience. You can also connect with others through your words. But amid all this, it's perfectly fine for you to be alone every once in a while.

Sun in the eleventh house: It's easy for you to relate to others, and they'll come to you when they need a shoulder to cry on. Helping people gives your life purpose, and achieving goals gives you satisfaction. You're very "people" oriented right now.

Sun in the twelfth house: It's time for self-reflection and introspection. You take time off by yourself, whether at home or elsewhere, so you can fully explore the depths of your mind and soul.

Moon

Moon in the first house: You're very passionate and emotional. You're the first to know when you're feeling down, and you own your feelings without caring what others think. Your emotions highly impact how you take care of yourself.

Moon in the second house: Your emotional state affects how much money you spend, so knowing how to gauge or balance your moods is important. You could learn to be more frugal with yourself.

Moon in the third house: There's nothing like comfort food to give you a sense of security. You're very loyal to your friends, and their friendship is important. You clearly understand what makes someone happy and what doesn't, so it's easy for you to judge other people on their happiness levels.

Moon in the fourth house: If you haven't already started doing it, consider getting a pet. There's a strong emotional connection between you and your pets, especially because they're loyal to their master. This is also the house of family and home, so take good care of both. You're very passionate about love and romance, and don't hide it from anyone. Your ambitions drive you.

Moon in the fifth house: You have many friends and acquaintances, and you can relate to anyone. Those who care for you are bound to have a very special place in your heart. You have a knack for making others feel comfortable.

Moon in the sixth house: You're empathetic and feel other people's feelings. You're also sensitive to criticism. But even though you have a knack for helping others, someone has to be there for you as much as everyone else.

Moon in the seventh house: You're very observant. When judging others, you don't just jump to conclusions. You consider all the evidence before concluding. This is the house of healing, so if there's anything that ails you, do whatever it takes to make yourself feel better. You care a lot about your family and friends, but you're also very self-sufficient. You can handle yourself without the help of anyone in love and romance.

Moon in the eighth house: You're emotional, passionate, and possessive in romantic relationships. It may be tough to find the right person who understands you, but at least you know you can balance your emotional state by being alone. You feel safe and secure in your home.

Moon in the ninth house: You're very intuitive and have a keen way of taking things apart to see what they're made of. You're also very romantic, and it's always a great time for romance and love. People who live with you are bound to feel safe and secure, especially in romance.

Moon in the tenth house: You're a very social person, so your connections with others are pretty strong. You may meet unfamiliar people at work or through your community activities, so be actively open to new people.

Moon in the eleventh house: You're very popular, and you can connect with everyone in one swoop. You have many friends, including acquaintances and even strangers, who are kind to you. If you're feeling lonely or down, many will comfort you.

Moon in the twelfth house: You are very introspective and reflective about your life. You start asking yourself questions about what makes your life meaningful and where you go from here. It's time for you to leave that place for a better place—yourself.

Mercury

Mercury in the first house: You think and talk very fast, so naturally, you're clever. You're ready to take on the world at a moment's notice. You like to be in the spotlight, and it's easy to stick out in a crowd.

Mercury in the second house: Your mind is always working at 100%, so you can't sit and relax. You have plenty of ideas often occurring simultaneously, but there's nothing worse than having nothing to do.

Mercury in the third house: One way or another, your words always get out into the world through phone calls or texting with friends, work colleagues, or family members.

Mercury in the fourth house: Your mind is always working, and you have a knack for making connections that make sense. You're also very patient, observant, and methodical in your approach to problems.

Mercury in the fifth house: Your communication skills are strong, so it's no surprise you're good with everyone, even children and animals. You're very entertaining and have a way of making people laugh.

Mercury in the sixth house: You're very imaginative and creative, always thinking of new ways to make a living or an income. You're also good at making money, though in your own methods.

Mercury in the seventh house: You're very interested in learning more, so you're quick to pick up new skills when they come along. You're an excellent communicator, and you'll make a great lawyer or teacher.

Mercury in the eighth house: You are a good listener and know how to get information out of someone without making them feel uncomfortable. You also have a knack for learning how and why people act the way they do and use the knowledge wisely.

Mercury in the ninth house: You're curious about life, so you always have new things to learn. Your intellect is sharp, and your mind never works at less than 100%. Your interests are varied, and you're always interested in what's going on.

Mercury in the tenth house: You talk a lot, but you hate it when other people give their input without knowing the full story. Talking is your way of obtaining more information. Talking with someone who asks questions that prompt your thoughts and feelings is best for you.

Mercury in the eleventh house: You have a way of making connections with people and people like you. You're good at presenting your point of view so they can understand. You have a knack for communicating with children, but be careful not to break their trust or treat them without cause.

Mercury in the twelfth house: You're very curious about life, and this curiosity helps you connect with people. But with romantic relationships, too much curiosity leads to deception or betrayal. Be careful of others' motives from now on. It's best to rely on more concrete information than your instincts when choosing a partner in love and romance.

Venus

Venus in the first house: You have a wonderful time with friends and are also very good at talking to friends and family. You'll find yourself in trouble if you fall out of love with people. You like to keep friendships, but don't forget to put your own needs first.

Venus in the second house: You enjoy being around friends, so this is an excellent time for socializing and making new connections. This is a very friendly planet, so you'll be popular wherever you go. As long as you know how to relax, it's easy to find the right balance between work and play in your daily activities.

Venus in the third house: Your relationships often seem unreal compared with your work life. You get involved with people more emotionally than you should. You're also very honest and straightforward, so you can't stop yourself from speaking your mind and being completely honest.

Venus in the fourth house: Your desire for harmony makes your friendships perfect for inner peace and stability. You never want anything to change. However, the rest of the world is moving forward rapidly, so keep up with the times.

Venus in the fifth house: Your friendships are highly important, and you're very nurturing and supportive of others. However, you know how to take care of yourself, including your needs. You would gain a lot from starting a relationship with someone who has a lot in common.

Venus in the sixth house: You think about your problems and how to solve them in various ways, so naturally, you're good at making connections between thoughts and ideas. Keep an open mind about what you learn about yourself and other people.

Venus in the seventh house: You're optimistic about your future, so you have a good chance of starting a positive new relationship during this period. You also have a knack for telling others what they need to hear to keep up with their lives and treat them well.

Venus in the eighth house: There's an emotional connection with people, making it easy for you to connect and understand people's emotions. But, if you do too much, it could lead to deception or betrayal with your partner in love or business.

Venus in the ninth house: You may develop a strong desire to travel or learn more about other cultures. You're excellent at making friends and can talk to anyone, even strangers. Your curiosity about other people and situations leads to a greater understanding of how things work in the world.

Venus in the tenth house: Your social life is very important, so you want to spend time with friends and family. Going out for entertainment becomes more important than staying home alone. You need friendly support from others, but make sure the people around you are on your side, not only after material advantages.

Venus in the eleventh house: You'll meet someone who shares your interests and will be a good friend. You'll enjoy talking with people and often feel like being with your friends more than anything. Talking with someone who asks questions that prompt your thoughts and feelings is best for you.

Venus in the twelfth house: You have a strong emotional bond with family or close friends, so it's not practical to take on any new responsibilities. Travel also helps you learn more about yourself but ensure you don't overlook important responsibilities at home. Don't let others' needs affect yours too strongly during this period.

Mars

Mars in the first house: You have a competitive nature. You want to win every argument, and you don't like losing. You're also quite determined, and you have an eye for detail in your career and other important activities. Watch out for accidents, injuries, or illnesses while traveling.

Mars in the second house: There's certainly no lack of energy with you, so you love doing physical activities with friends and family. You're also very clear about what's in your best interests with money and possessions. However, if you don't take care of yourself, it could lead to trouble.

Mars in the third house: It's important to have fun with friends, relatives, and even strangers. You're very aggressive, but that's not necessarily a bad thing. Fight your own battles whenever you have an argument or a conflict, and don't let others take advantage of you.

Mars in the fourth house: Mars energy helps you decide more quickly. You can achieve more things than normal if you work hard enough. Feeling good about yourself is important for helping others feel good about themselves.

Mars in the fifth house: Your competitive nature could lead to arguments, especially with people you're close to. You feel competitive with others and have a strong will to succeed. There's also an attraction to people doing well financially.

Mars in the sixth house: You like being around friends or your romantic partner. Guard your health and finances firmly because it's important to be healthy and wealthy. You need to be careful with spending money on luxury items. It's imperative to live within your means.

Mars in the seventh house: You have an active social life, which can be very positive when well-led and organized. You're excellent at making friends, officiating at parties, and hosting activities to help people get to know each other better.

Mars in the eighth house: You strongly crave material gain, so often take on more responsibility than you can handle. You also spend too much money or even get involved in financial fraud and embezzlement. You need to control your anger and aggression or risk going to jail.

Mars in the ninth house: Your desire to learn more about the world by traveling is very strong. You enjoy learning about everything from travel to food to people's activities in different regions. You're good at making friends, even if others don't realize it at first.

Mars in the tenth house: There's a strong desire to spend time with people and not only for social reasons. You need to invest your time in friends and family. You feel a strong need to earn money if you're out of work. Doing something that keeps you actively involved in the world is best for you.

Mars in the eleventh house: Your desire for action is apparent, and you like having fun and talking about interesting things with friends. You can enjoy spoken or written debates when someone makes a logical argument on an issue or topic that interests both parties.

Mars in the twelfth house: You are secretive or even deceptive with your plans and ideas, so don't expect others to understand where you want to go or what you want to do with your life unless you are open with them.

Jupiter

Jupiter in the first house: You are a friendly and optimistic person who enjoys spending time with friends. You like being a role model for younger people and a mentor or teacher. Spending time outdoors as much as possible is best for you.

Jupiter in the second house: You are generous with your wealth and ensure that family members are taken care of financially. The circumstances around you lead to financial opportunities, but it's best to live within your means.

Jupiter in the third house: You have a very outgoing personality and enjoy talking with people about anything. You're quite social and get along with everyone easily. You're also intelligent and could be a teacher or academic.

Jupiter in the fourth house: You have a strong family bond and enjoy spending time with relatives and people you're close to. Overlooked activities like home improvement projects could give you a boost in energy that lasts for many days.

Jupiter in the fifth house: You want nothing more than to be with your partner, spouse, or children, and it's important to spend more time together. Your interest in sports is strong, and there's an attraction to outdoor activities like golf or tennis. Spending time enjoying yourself with other people is best.

Jupiter in the sixth house: Your sense of humor is strong, and you enjoy laughing and joking with people. You could be a teacher or work for a charity. Some concern must be given to travel or relocating plans in the near future because it could affect your work.

Jupiter in the seventh house: You love being with your partner or spouse, and it's important to spend more time together. You're also very friendly and enjoy helping others solve problems they have difficulty dealing with independently.

Jupiter in the eighth house: You have an optimistic and positive outlook on life and like being around active people. There's an attraction to the elderly, especially if they're active. You may deal with health issues, but you can lead a very healthy lifestyle with good nutrition, exercise, and a positive attitude.

Jupiter in the ninth house: Your desire to learn more about the world is strong, as is your interest in philosophy or astronomy. You enjoy talking with people who care about far-reaching topics larger than life or even small topics like gossip. Spend time traveling and possibly attending lectures or classes at a college.

Jupiter in the tenth house: You like being active and can get along with almost everyone. You might want to be a public figure or performer. You do very well in the arts and academic fields considered liberal arts – like writing and philosophy.

Jupiter in the eleventh house: Your desire to help others is very strong. You like talking with people who have individualistic ideas and are open to new things. You might travel or work with people with similar interests.

Jupiter in the twelfth house: Others recognize your desire to help them when they need advice for life situations. There's an attraction to scientific studies and people interested in the occult or psychic practices.

Saturn

Saturn in the first house: Your desire to be an authority is strong, and you enjoy being a role model for others. There's an attraction to philosophy and an academic field with very strict standards.

Saturn in the second house: You are a bit of a perfectionist. You worry about spending too much money. However, you handle money responsibly and will likely have many savings for your retirement years.

Saturn in the third house: Your ability to learn is excellent, and you're an avid reader of books or magazines that contain interesting facts or teach you something new. You like to teach others about the world around them.

Saturn in the fourth house: You enjoy being with people and are quite social. You enjoy being around others in groups and talking about your interests. Your need to be involved in traveling activities is strong, and you have an adventurous spirit.

Saturn in the fifth house: You handle money responsibly but are not particularly generous in sharing your wealth or helping family members financially. There is a higher probability of illness related to health issues like joints, bones, or skin.

Saturn in the sixth house: You love to be of service and choose to work in a service-oriented industry, like teaching or helping those having difficulty getting around. You may deal with health issues, but you can manage your symptoms effectively with proper nutrition and exercise.

Saturn in the seventh house: You have an attraction to older people you admire or share similar interests and possibly an attraction to someone already married. However, it's best to spend time with someone you love and who loves you back.

Saturn in the eighth house: You handle money responsibly, but there's a higher probability of being involved in legal matters, like contracts and legal settlements. There's an attraction to risky or taboo activities, like gambling or even illegal activities.

Saturn in the ninth house: Your desire to learn more about the world is strong, and you enjoy learning from books or lectures by people with great knowledge. You could work for someone well-known and respected for their skills. Keep an open mind about your beliefs, and don't be so closed off to people's ideas.

Saturn in the tenth house: You are drawn to authority figures and love to be a mentor or someone looked up to. You set the best examples for those following in your footsteps.

Saturn in the eleventh house: Your desire to be helpful is strong, and you enjoy mentoring others, especially younger people. You could teach at a college or university or teach other people new life lessons.

Saturn in the twelfth house: Your need to be involved with travel activities involving travel and having visitors is strong. But there's also an attraction to strange subjects and people fascinated with the occult or psychic practices.

Uranus

Uranus in the first house: You love to be different and are quite eccentric. There's an attraction to unusual or controversial subjects that people appreciate, and you've done much research on those subjects. You're creative, innovative, and freedom-loving.

Uranus in the second house: You dislike routine and have a strong desire to explore the world. There's also an attraction to the new subject matter, since what interests you is new and different each day. You're also innovative and free-thinking.

Uranus in the third house: You have a knack for discovering secrets and would enjoy traveling through space. If you're lucky, you'll work for NASA or a similar organization. You like being different, which attracts quirky or eccentric people. There is an attraction to older people who know subjects that interest you.

Uranus in the fourth house: You're very creative and unconventional and have a strong desire to seek fame or money from your ideas that others might appreciate. You could be involved in the arts. However, spending time with someone you love and who loves you back is best.

Uranus in the fifth house: You don't like regular routines or repeating the same activities each day. You have an unusual desire to travel to other countries and learn about their customs. There's a higher probability of you having health issues related to your bones, joints, or skin.

Uranus in the sixth house: You're innovative and unconventional, but your desire to be different also attracts you to bizarre subjects others might find humorous. Be open-minded about religions, philosophies, and politics.

Uranus in the seventh house: You handle money responsibly, but there's a higher probability of being involved in legal matters related to contracts or settlements. You could be involved in the arts and be a performer, an actor, or even a director.

Uranus in the eighth house: Your desire to be different is strong, but there's also an attraction to unusual or controversial subjects people appreciate. You're creative and innovative.

Uranus in the ninth house: You love to learn new things and enjoy learning new life lessons. You could work for someone, like teaching or mentoring. Keep an open mind about other people's beliefs, and don't be so closed off to your ideas.

Uranus in the tenth house: You have an unusual desire to be different and unconventional. There's a higher probability of being involved in legal matters like contracts, contracts, or settlements. You could be involved with the arts, like acting, directing, or even writing.

Uranus in the eleventh house: You crave authenticity and originality. If you go against society's expectations, you could get into trouble with the law or out of place among your peers. Stay true to yourself, and don't sacrifice who you truly are for anyone else's expectations.

Uranus in the twelfth house: You're different and unconventional, and there's also an attraction to strange people and occult practices. You could be involved with the arts or work for someone with connections with people from other cultures.

Neptune

Neptune in the first house: Your need to be different is strong, but you also want to rebel or explore new things. You could become involved in various mysticism and alternative religions contrary to what your family or other members of society believe. There's an attraction to unusual subjects like occult practices, astrology, and fortune-telling.

Neptune in the second house: You have your own ideas about handling money. You're creative and have many original ideas, but there's an attraction to unusual subjects like occult practices, astrology, and fortune-telling.

Neptune in the third house: You are a person who loves to explore new subjects, especially those controversial or even illegal. You may be drawn to subjects relating to the arts or theater.

Neptune in the fourth house: Your desire to be different and rebel against your family's expectations is strong. However, you are also attracted to paranormal things like horoscopes, fortune-telling, or other divination. There is an attraction to older people with knowledge about subjects that interest you.

Neptune in the fifth house: Your desire to be different and explore new subjects could become a problem because you may receive negative reactions from others. Your curiosity about many subjects also attracts eccentric people who have unusual practices.

Neptune in the sixth house: You're drawn to discovering secrets and mysteries, but there's also an attraction to unusual subjects like occult practices, astrology, and fortune-telling. You could be involved with the arts or even videos, movies, or dramas, dabbling in genres concerning the ethereal.

Neptune in the seventh house: You enjoy new places and explore different things, driven by your desire to be involved with occult practices from all over the map. You could also be involved in the arts or even letters, magazines, or books.

Neptune in the eighth house: Your interest in things that are outside the conventional could make you vulnerable to scams or negative energy. You may be involved in businesses related to the occult, like astrology or divination.

Neptune in the ninth house: You could become confused about who you truly are as you explore different topics because so much information and influence are coming in your direction. Keep an open mind about life and other people's feelings, beliefs, and emotions.

Neptune in the tenth house: Your mind is open to new ideas and has many original ideas. You could be involved in the arts or even more unusual subjects, like astrology or divination.

Neptune in the eleventh house: You have an attraction to unconventional people. There's also a chance you could want to live in a dreamy world where reality takes second place to your fantasies. Keep an open mind about people who are different and don't judge them for their different beliefs.

Neptune in the twelfth house: There's a higher probability of being involved with occult practices, mystical beliefs, and other superstitious practices. It's also possible that you suddenly become attracted to the supernatural or astrology.

Pluto

Pluto in the first house: You're different from other people, but there's also a higher probability of being involved with drugs or illegal substances. You could be a drug dealer or even work for someone with connections to people who deal drugs. Keep an open mind about life and people's opinions instead of being closed off to your ideas.

Pluto in the second house: You have a strong desire to be different and rebel against being forced to do things you don't want to do. Keep an open mind about life and other people's feel, beliefs, and emotions.

Pluto in the third house: There's a high probability of becoming involved with drugs, illegal substances, or even occult practices, particularly astrology or palm reading. You could also be involved with arts, like music, painting, or writing.

Pluto in the fourth house: You have a strong desire to be different and rebel against being forced to do things you don't want to do. You could also be involved with illegal activities like drugs or gambling, or even work with illegal aspects, like a drug weapons dealer.

Pluto in the fifth house: There's a high probability of becoming involved in drugs, occult practices, or other illegal activities. The difficulty is that you have to learn the hard way that these activities will hurt you more than they help.

Pluto in the sixth house: You could be the perfect candidate for any illegal activity or drug dealing, so be careful. Keep an open mind about life and people's feelings, beliefs, and emotions.

Pluto in the seventh house: You are interested in occult practices and things against conservative rules. So, keep an open mind about life and other people's feelings, beliefs, and emotions.

Pluto in the eighth house: There's a strong desire to be different and rebel against being forced to do things you don't want to do. You're also attracted to the universe's dark side, like illegal drugs and other negative influences.

Pluto in the ninth house: You are interested in occult practices and things against conservative rules. Keep an open mind about life and other people's feelings, beliefs, and emotions.

Pluto in the tenth house: You love to find out information about other people's lives and learn why they do the things they do. Your mind is open to new ideas and has many original ideas. You could also become involved in political groups or organizations with a social conscience or moral code.

Pluto in the eleventh house: You have an attraction to unconventional people. There's also a chance you could want to live in a dreamy world where reality takes second place to your fantasies.

Pluto in the twelfth house: More than anyone, you are attracted to the supernatural, particularly astrology. The difficulty is that the fantasy becomes a reality and could negatively take over your life, so watch out.

Chapter 7: The Influence of Moon Phases

Moon phases.
https://www.pexels.com/photo/timelapse-photography-of-moon-1275413/

While the sun may take center stage, we can't ignore the moon's influence on our personalities in astrology. The moon represents the energy that prevails throughout our day, and it lets you know what you need to do to feel good enough to accomplish your life mission. It helps you with your goals, but keep in mind that you feel you're embodying more of your true self because it focuses on your emotional life, which is essential to your overall well-being.

The New Moon

The new moon is the most important of all phases. There's no illumination, and during this phase, all of your dreams are realized if you are lucky. An old Spanish superstition states that catching a new moon reflection on a mirror in total darkness will bring luck. Even if the person doesn't know what they are doing or has no idea how to use it, because of its association with luck and changes in your life, that luck will happen

What does the new moon represent? The new moon represents the beginning of a journey, a fresh start, and a time when you could accomplish anything. It's an excellent time to initiate new beginnings and make big plans for the future. It could be an important part of your long-term planning, especially if you are daring and risk-taking, like starting a business or traveling to a foreign country by yourself. By doing this, you are allowing yourself to change your life around.

What does the new moon mean for your relationships? You should be in a new relationship during the new moon phase as this gives you the chance to start afresh with your partner. Be very open and tell your partner all of your emotions, as this will build trust between you. It's also worth remembering that the new moon means fresh starts and life changes. Therefore, if you have been with your partner for a while and things are wearing thin, it's best to start looking for a new relationship or putting in some effort to make it feel new.

What does the new moon mean for your relationship with yourself? The new moon offers a good time to work on yourself and make changes. Also, think about what you want from your life. You may find the new moon offers you the chance to start afresh.

Self-love Tips for the New Moon

1. Talk to yourself. Talk to your "inner self" – the one speaking at night when you feel most alone. Ask this inner voice what it has to say and listen carefully.

2. Give yourself little slices of happiness: You may focus too much on the negative aspects of your life, so make time for a nice moment or treat yourself, take some pressure off, and it could be very uplifting. A little treat can make all the difference to feeling happy about life or setting an intention for success in the coming month.

3. Don't hold back on the compliments: It's important to compliment yourself because being critical of your self-esteem can negatively affect your mental health. Don't be afraid to take time out of the day to sit and think about what you are doing well.

Dating Tips for the New Moon

1. Take a risk: The new moon is great for taking risks in love. However, it can also encourage you to stray from good practices, so think twice before going ahead. But, if things seem right and you're sure, take that risk. You could be pleasantly surprised.

2. Let your emotions flow: There is a time during the new moon phase when your emotions are not as intense as they could be, so take this opportunity to let your emotions flow and be open about how you feel with someone you want to get close to.

3. Be open: Don't bury your emotions because the moon's light makes it easier to see what you need to see.

Relationship advice for the new moon: This is a good time to renew your vows and commitment to each other.

The Waxing Crescent Moon

When the moon creates the shape of a crescent, this is the phase when you experience a lot of transformation and loads of chances for new things in your life.

What does the waxing crescent moon represent? During this phase, you'll feel most energetic and accomplish all you desire. It symbolizes the idea of growth and being in control of your surroundings and situation. Concentrate on your goals and make plans for the long term, as it will help you.

What does the waxing crescent moon mean for your relationships? The waxing crescent moon is when things are intensifying and heating up. You start to feel more romantic or have an increased sex drive, and while this is when you are likely to be the most decisive person in your relationship, it also leaves you feeling overeager. You have a hard time saying no and will probably just say yes to any request, regardless of what it is. The waxing crescent moon also signifies the start of a new cycle when taking risks can have positive consequences and reward you. However, this moon cycle only lasts a few days to a week.

What does the waxing crescent moon mean for your relationship with yourself? The waxing crescent moon means that you give yourself permission to be fully loved and known as you open up to love and intimacy. The waxing crescent moon symbolizes the first signs of a new cycle. This cycle is about opening up and being more intimate with yourself. You may notice you have more patience with your flaws and are more forgiving of yourself when you make mistakes. This is a time when you're born again. The energy of this moon sets up new feelings and habits toward yourself and leaves old feelings and habits behind. These feelings can be mixed, but it's mainly being born again after something traumatic or painful has happened.

Self-Love Tips for the Waxing Crescent Moon

1. Treat yourself to a massage. The waxing crescent moon is a great time to pamper yourself and treat yourself to something nice. Schedule a massage or a pedicure to feel more relaxed.

2. Erase negative self-talk. One of the ways you can love yourself more easily is by giving up negative self-talk and replacing it with positive statements about who you are and how your life is going. Practicing gratitude every day is especially helpful if you're having difficulty practicing self-love on the waxing crescent moon.

3. Be forgiving with yourself if mistakes are made or if there are changes in your routine or schedule during the waxing crescent moon cycle.

Dating Tips for the Waxing Crescent Moon

1. The waxing crescent moon is a good time to get out and meet new people. You may be more assertive and more willing to take risks during this time, so you're likely to make friends or meet potential dates at social events.

2. This phase can make you feel slightly impatient in relationships, so if you're currently dating someone, don't get too annoyed or frustrated when they aren't moving as quickly as you want.

3. This is a good time for flirting but not a great time for starting serious relationships with people who seem uninterested in you or highly negative about your feelings for them.

Relationship advice for the waxing crescent moon: If your relationship is only starting, be very mindful about nurturing it.

The First Quarter Moon

At this point, more than a crescent of the moon is illuminated. There's even more stirring in yourself for new things picking up steam.

What does the first quarter moon represent? This is a time for setting things in motion when people feel impatient, restless, and hungry for change. People experience a need to get things started and put plans into place during the first quarter moon. It also symbolizes slowing down and action that has already been taken. A new cycle begins as the moon goes from darkness into light. There's a big push and pull between what you want to do versus what you should be doing to achieve your goals. Now is the time to set things in motion, like a new job or your own business.

What does the first quarter moon mean for your relationship? The first quarter moon is when you are likely to be more intelligent and focused than usual. You feel assertive and in control of your life — but it makes you more impatient than usual with who you're involved with. People on the first quarter moon will often develop strong opinions about various issues and feel stronger about them, whether they're right or wrong. The first quarter moon is a turning point in the road. Things that were once just words or thoughts become actions and eventually come together as a solid reality.

What does the first quarter moon mean for your relationship with yourself? The first quarter moon is a time for being more objective about your feelings and thoughts about life. You notice you have more patience for other people's mistakes and shortcomings, but not for yourself. You see yourself with a harsh eye or overly critical of things you do or say. At this time, be patient with yourself as you are with those around you. Be kinder to yourself to start the new phase of the waxing crescent moon cycle on a positive note. It helps if you write down what you want to change and look at it objectively before making plans to change it.

Self-love Tips for the First Quarter Moon

1. As you feel more in charge of your life, you have more patience with yourself and others. This is when you pace yourself and ask for help when needed. Treating yourself to something special helps bring about this change.

2. Avoid being too hard on yourself every day about your weight, hair, or clothes in the first quarter moon cycle. It's okay not to feel perfect all the time during this cycle.

3. Avoid watching television or movies that show people being hurt, ridiculed, or humiliated.

4. If you find yourself in a tight spot, like not having enough money to live on and choosing between paying your rent and taking out loans, be aware that this time is about setting plans in motion for the future, so a better day is coming soon.

Dating Tips for the First Quarter Moon

1. The first quarter moon is a good time for trying out new things, so dating could be a lot of fun during this time.

2. This cycle is about setting plans into motion, so if you're thinking of asking someone out or getting more serious in general, wait until later in the cycle when you pass the half-moon phase.

3. It is a good time for flirting and not unusual to find others falling in love with you. If you're already dating or have interests besides finding love, avoid being aggressive or overly flirtatious during this moon phase.

Relationship advice for the first quarter moon: The first quarter moon is a time to be assertive, but be patient. It's natural to feel impatient and want things to happen faster than they do. But it's essential not to make this a habit so that you don't lose the love you have.

The Waxing Gibbous Moon

The only part of the moon that isn't illuminated is the crescent. It's more than half-lit but not quite fully so.

What does the waxing gibbous moon represent? The gibbous moon represents things that are still new just before a full moon when people experience a surge of optimism and enthusiasm. During the gibbous moon, people feel they are getting close to what they want to achieve in life. They get closer and closer to their goals until, eventually, it is all realized or achieved at the full moon. This cycle's phase is important because it prepares you for future achievements and changes. This aspect of life makes everything seem more worthwhile, but many people have problems staying focused on one activity or thought for too long during this cycle due to wanting so much out of life.

What does the waxing gibbous moon mean for your relationship? This is a challenging cycle for people involved in new relationships because it's not always easy to balance being positive about your relationship and wanting things to happen quickly. If you feel your relationship is not moving fast enough, it will negatively affect the person. It's essential not to shut them out if you want the relationship to work out.

What does the waxing gibbous moon mean for your relationship with yourself? You notice you get excited about your future experiences during this cycle, even if nothing has happened yet. This is when many people make plans to travel or focus on new and different things in their lives. For some people, this cycle is also when they confirm wanting to remain on their career path. They are certain there's no other way to be happy, making it difficult to adapt later in life if they change jobs or careers.

Self-Love Tips for the Waxing Gibbous Moon

1. The gibbous moon is a time to enjoy your life, so make the most of it.
2. This is a good cycle for planning out the next few weeks or months of your life.
3. You may feel like eating more than usual during this cycle and crave salty foods.
4. For people who have trouble sleeping during this time, keeping a journal on their nightstand to write down their thoughts at the end of each day will help clear their minds when they go to sleep.

Dating Tips for the Waxing Gibbous Moon

1. The gibbous moon is a good cycle to use when you want to ask someone out, but it's also a good time to settle into a relationship that has been going well.
2. This is the most romantic phase, so you should reveal more of your feelings than usual and let yourself be vulnerable.
3. If you're thinking about breaking up with someone or if they want this to happen too, don't do it during this cycle.

Relationship advice for the waxing gibbous moon: The gibbous moon is a good time for being creative and cautious about your plans. When you plan something new, it's important to think it through and not rush into anything. It's also important to be open to change and the unpredictable.

The Full Moon

When the moon is full, it shines high in the sky and is surrounded by darkness. It's fully illuminated.

What does the full moon represent? This is when people feel they have everything they want in life, although it's only a peak experience before the descent back to reality. It's important to enjoy this stage of life while it lasts because there are many steps to achieve long-term results after this period. This stage of life represents the reality of your goals and how they match up with where you are right now. For some people, reaching this stage isn't always pleasant because it shows what's missing in their lives or how far away they still are from realizing their dreams.

What does the full moon mean for your relationship? Love is strongest during this phase, so it's imperative to enjoy this time in your relationship and allow yourself to be vulnerable even if you have doubts.

What does the full moon mean for your relationship with yourself? Since the full moon is a time of balance and achievement, obtaining long-term success and happiness, it's important to not just focus on one or two areas of your life. In particular, don't become too focused on one career or subject for too long. You'll probably experience setbacks in this stage of life, so you mustn't be too attached to things that no longer serve you.

Self-love Tips for the Full Moon

1. You desire to be more creative and expressive during this cycle, so do something creative.

2. There is a powerful temptation to give up and give in to your emotions. Don't do it. This is a time when many people want things to happen very quickly. However, these cycles aren't about experiencing positive or negative events. They are about learning lessons about what's most important in your life and how you deal with challenges.

3. Some people feel they have to live up to high expectations, but it's important not to be so unrealistic about what you think you can achieve.

Dating Tips for the Full Moon

1. This is a good time to be more romantic and expressive with your partner, but don't overdo it, or you can become too needy.

2. When you're on a date, it's important to be on the same wavelength as your date.

3. It's also a good time to make plans for meeting people if this is what you want to do.

Relationship advice for the full moon: It's important not to assume that others will be ready for the effort needed to get things started in your relationship. Hold back until you're both sure these are the right steps.

The Waning Gibbous Moon

This moon is almost full, and you'll see it about three to five days after the full moon.

What does the waning gibbous moon represent? The waning gibbous moon is when people feel more alert and energized than usual. It is also a time of restlessness and boredom because the mind is not stimulated. It is a good time for people to feel like they're living in their comfort zone to take on some new challenges at work or in relationships.

What does the waning gibbous moon mean for your relationship? For people living in their comfort zone, the waning gibbous moon will be a time to relax and let go of many responsibilities. It is a great time to make changes in your life if you're looking for a break.

What does the waning gibbous moon mean for your relationship with yourself? During this moon stage, you're stuck in a rut, and there's nothing new or exciting you can do to change things for yourself. If you want to alter your life for the better somehow, it's best to wait until your dream phase starts because then you'll have more motivation for change.

Self-Love Tips for the Waning Gibbous Moon

1. This is a good time to take a break from many responsibilities, especially if you feel trapped.

2. If you have been waiting for something new to happen in your life, now is a good time to try something new and different.

3. Don't focus on your fears or concerns for the future. Your purpose may be unclear at this point in your life, so it's important

not to get too caught up in where things are going.

Dating Tips for the Waning Gibbous Moon

1. For those who are single, this is a good time to rest and relax without feelings of guilt or pressure.

2. For people in committed relationships, it's important not to use this cycle as an excuse to ignore personal responsibilities. Many couples take advantage of each other during this cycle, so spend some time alone instead during the waning gibbous moon so that you don't feel taken advantage of.

3. This is a powerful phrase for people who may be thinking about divorce.

Relationship advice for the waning gibbous moon: Refuse to let your fears control you. If you're too fearful of the future, this is not a good time to make any big changes in relationships. Instead, take some time for yourself during this cycle and recharge your batteries.

The Last Quarter Moon

This is the phase just before the waning crescent phase. It is a time for completion, moving on from something, and reorienting yourself. It's a time to wrap things up, especially whatever you began during the new moon phase.

What does the last quarter moon represent? During this moon phase, it's important not to have unrealistic expectations about what another person could be like for you. If you're going through a rough time in your life, it's best to wait until the full moon phase before trying to change things.

What does the last quarter moon represent for your relationship with yourself? If you're feeling stagnant in your life, it's important not to expect too much from yourself during this time since it's more difficult to feel the sense of connectedness needed for growth. If you feel like things are out of balance in your life, wait until the full moon phase to make changes.

What does the last quarter moon represent for relationships? This is a powerful time for decision-making about relationships because it's a highly charged phase. You should wait until the full moon phase before ending a relationship or deciding on your next step in life.

Self-Love Tips for the Last Quarter Moon

1. As this is a symbolic phase for endings and new beginnings, it's a good time for taking care of any unfinished work on your plate over the past month or two.

2. This is a good time for single people to focus less on finding someone new and more on self-improvement.

3. For those in common-law relationships, it's a good time to take some time for yourself to focus on your emotional needs instead of keeping things in the background for your partner.

Dating Tips for the Last Quarter Moon

1. During this phase of the moon, it's important to spend time alone to reflect and give attention to your needs.

2. For those in a relationship, it's best not to break up or start something new during this cycle because you will be too busy taking care of your needs.

3. For those who are single, it's best not to look for a date during this cycle because you need time for yourself right now.

Relationship advice for the last quarter moon: Your next steps in life may be unclear right now, so it's best not to make any major life decisions during this phase. This is a time for taking care of unfinished business and wrapping up loose ends in your life, especially in your relationship with yourself.

The Waning Crescent Moon

This is the final phase of the moon, where just a crescent is lit. It is a time to get to know yourself and accept who you are. It's the best time to release all the things that no longer serve you and embrace love instead.

What does the waning crescent moon represent? The waning crescent moon is a time of self-acceptance and self-love. It's a time to learn how to love yourself to better connect with others.

What does the waning crescent moon represent for your relationship with yourself? During this phase of the moon, you have the power to eliminate fears getting in the way so that you can move forward. If you feel something holding you back in your life, now is the time to figure out what it is and work through it so you no longer feel fearful when it comes up again. If you're feeling stagnant or held back from fulfilling your dreams and doing what makes you happy, this moon phase will help bring balance to your life by eliminating what's holding you back.

What does the waning crescent moon represent for your relationships? If you're in a relationship, you can see what keeps you from feeling close to them. If your marriage is on the rocks, this is a great time to resolve the problems so that you don't lose something dear to your heart. Listen carefully to what others are saying and make sure they say things aligned with how you want to live your life. If not, it may be time for some changes.

Self-Love Tips for the Waning Crescent Moon

1. For those who are single, this is a good time to take time for yourself to focus on loving yourself.

2. It will be easier to find someone new as long as you keep things light and fun and don't pressure yourself while looking for a date or mate.

3. Let go of unhealthy relationships and friends so that you can embrace more love and happiness in your life.

Dating Tips for the Waning Crescent Moon

1. If you're single, this is a great time for meeting new people.

2. It will be easier for those not currently in a relationship to attract new people during this cycle because you have more self-love and confidence in yourself than at other times of the month.

3. It may be appropriate for those currently in a relationship to look for someone new or end the relationship during this cycle because you have more love and confidence in yourself than at other times of the month.

Relationship advice for the waning crescent moon: This is a powerful time for removing things from your life so you can embrace more love and happiness. This is a symbolically charged phase, so it's important to ensure that what you do reflects your true beliefs about love and happiness in your life.

Chapter 8: A Guide to Twin Flames

What are twin flames? The concept of twin flames has been around for thousands of years, but the term has only recently become common usage. It is a powerful and beautiful idea that has finally achieved wide recognition. If you ask anyone about twin flames these days, the chances they'll at least have heard about them in passing.

The term "twin flame" refers to two souls who have come into this world to experience togetherness and intimacy on a level most people never get to experience in their entire lives. Twin flames are two halves of the same soul that have found each other again, but this time with the awareness to love and care for one another.

Twin Flames and Spiritual Astrology

Using astrology to explore how twin flames manifest in our world is a very important but often overlooked understanding of the nature of twin flames. Astrology is used to help form an understanding of what they are and represent. The basic idea behind twin flame relationships is that your soul's journey on Earth has a purpose beyond your goals or destiny. By studying the natal charts of each person in the twin flame relationship, astrologers can distinguish the traits and tendencies shared by both of you that are expressions of your soul's mission on Earth. They also help you achieve the goal you both agreed to in this incarnation.

Signs You've Met Your Twin Flame

1. Your connection is instant, deep, and profound.

2. Your backgrounds and interests are the same or very similar.

3. You both had the same strange thoughts and dreams about one another before you met.

4. You are involved with the same people for extended periods, even if not together.

5. You feel you've known each other for much longer than this lifetime or any lifetime before it.

6. You feel you're made for one another or have known each other your entire life.

7. You finish each other's sentences and know what the other will say before they've said it.

8. You communicate on a deep intuitive level without speaking a word and can even read each other's minds.

9. Your souls recognize one another as eternal companions, past and future, in many lifetimes and dimensions.

10. You're obsessed with one another. You're drawn to one another wherever you are, constantly in touch somehow even if you don't see each other regularly (due to distance).

11. You're inseparable. You can barely function or be happy without each other, even after just a short time together.

12. You learn many things about yourself through your twin, including your strengths and weaknesses.

13. Your connection to each other feels like home, the place you belong – as if you've found your true self in your twin flame.

14. Your inner wounds feel healed when you're with each other as if they never existed.

15. You feel complete when you're with one another, finally understanding who you are and where you belong in the world.

16. You feel like you can always talk to each other about anything, have everything in common, and get to know yourself better.

17. You feel at home when you're together, even if it is only for two hours.

18. Your connection feels like a deep, lifelong friendship or family bond between souls.

19. You feel your twin is the missing piece of your puzzle, the perfect *other half*, the best friend you've ever had, or the love of your life.

20. Your connection feels bigger than just two people. It's something much larger than your two souls existing independently of one another.

The Pros of a Twin Flame Relationship

1. A twin flame relationship helps you understand and accept your sexual and spiritual identity.

2. A twin flame relationship helps you break the chains of addictive relationships with other people and substances because it shows what true intimacy feels like.

3. A twin flame relationship helps you discover who you truly are, your purpose, life's passion, higher self (the most spiritual version of yourself), and much more.

4. You have a built-in best friend for life with a twin flame who is there for you regardless of what happens or where life takes you. They never leave your side, even in their physical absence from this world or dimension (if the relationship ends due to death).

5. Twin flame relationships are a gateway to personal growth and spiritual enlightenment because they're the best chance you get to learn about your past lives, karma, and soul purpose.

6. Twin flame relationships help you break from the shackles of this life to live a full life (even if only in spirit form) in the next.

7. A twin flame relationship helps you deeply connect with your higher self (the most spiritual version of yourself), your soul.

8. A twin flame relationship greatly helps you to heal any inner wounds that have kept you from fully receiving love and intimacy in your current life.

9. A twin flame relationship brings tremendous physical healing and a better quality of life relative to your well-being before the relationship came into your life.

10. You'll never feel you've wasted time being with your twin flame, even if you have to be separated from them for extended periods

or they die (if the relationship ends).

11. A twin flame relationship brings you comfort when nothing else can and reminds you there is always hope in this world when everything else is going wrong.

Cons of a Twin Flame Relationship

1. Twin flame relationships are exhausting because they pull you out of your normal consciousness level and make you live more at the moment than most people.

2. A twin flame relationship causes extreme emotional ups and downs because it splits your focus and attention among two people instead of one.

3. A twin flame relationship causes jealousy and possessiveness if you don't work to keep those emotions at bay or heal them through self-work.

4. It is hard to separate yourself from a twin flame when their problems spill over into your life. Everything becomes about them, their drama, or their issues (whether you like it or not).

5. It isn't easy to find time for yourself because everything is about your twin flame and the relationship. It is another form of codependency from that standpoint.

6. Twin flames put too much pressure on you to "figure it out" when you have no idea about what's going on or what you're doing.

7. Sometimes, it's hard to take care of yourself when you have a twin flame in your life. You have the potential to be taken advantage of, and your time and energy are sucked into something that doesn't matter, which leaves you feeling rejected.

8. A twin flame relationship keeps you from fully living in this lifetime because you're distracted by other things and neglect yourself or others around you.

9. A twin flame relationship causes unrequited love and a longer-than-usual process to get over the relationship when it ends.

10. A twin flame relationship makes you feel like you're running on an emotional rollercoaster, and no one understands what you're going through.

Challenges in a Twin Flame Relationship

1. You have to be in a place mentally and emotionally to handle the ups and downs of a twin flame relationship, meaning you have to be emotionally healthy (not codependent) and ready to handle the intensity of your twin's highs and lows.

2. You have to want this relationship in your life because it's not something everyone can handle. It takes a person who doesn't experience an adverse reaction to high emotional energy levels because they must learn to transmute them instead.

3. You have to be emotionally ready to deal with your twin's drama and issues, which might not always be appropriate or something you feel comfortable diving into. You have to be ready to separate yourself from their problems when they come into your life because they're not your own.

4. You have to handle all the attention that comes with a twin flame relationship, including the flack you may receive from other people who think you're crazy or insecure or it's just a phase you're going through.

5. You have to handle the intense feelings you experience with your twin flame and all that goes with it when they're absent from this dimension. Once you know that they're in a better place than with you, you'll know how to release the pent-up emotions and get on with life.

6. You have to be emotionally and mentally healthy enough for a twin flame relationship because it will take over your life or drain your energy.

7. You have to be ready for your twin flame relationship to change your life more than anything else in your current life.

8. You have to be ready to learn much more about yourself and your spirituality to gain the insights, knowledge, and skills to handle a twin flame relationship.

9. You have to be emotionally and mentally prepared for your twin flame relationship to end and the pain that goes with it.

10. You have to be ready for a twin flame relationship because once it starts, it will set off a chain of events in your life that you may not be prepared for.

Advice for Being in a Twin Flame Relationship

You must first open up to your intuition and listen to it regarding your twin flame relationship. It doesn't matter how much you deny it; you're meant for each other. Your twin flame relationship will show itself in many ways, so keep an open mind, heart, and spirit. Watch for signs that your connection is not as strong as it appears and is not a soul mate bond.

Even if you think you've found your twin flame already, keep looking. You could come across others who will teach you something about life and love, even if they're not your true twin flame.

Talk to trusted friends and family members who will give you an outside perspective on what's going on in your relationship with your twin flame. They will see things you don't because they're emotionally distant from the situation. Their feedback could clear confusion or uncertainty in the relationship. Let them know how important their insights are to you, so they will be more willing to share with you without being hesitant or afraid of being wrong.

Twin flame relationships aren't for everyone, so if you're not emotionally and mentally healthy enough to handle the intensity of one, it's best to steer clear altogether. The energy exchange will pressure your mental and emotional health, causing you to burn out or break down completely if you're not ready for this type of relationship—and sometimes, even if you are.

If your twin flame is deceased and has crossed over into the afterlife or another dimension, know that they're still with you (and always will be). This causes them to appear in dreams or visions, but these are merely ways they communicate with you without burdening your physical body with their energies.

Advice for Finding Your Twin Flame

1. Re-evaluate what love means to you. If the feeling of love and happiness is all around you abundantly, ask yourself who or what is responsible.
2. List the things missing in your life from the advice of others. Your twin flame will likely be the embodiment of all that's missing. Writing the list manifests to bring them to you.

3. Look at your life and the world around you, and ask yourself who's responsible for the beautiful things already in existence.

4. Look back on your past, and ask yourself what hurt or devastated you in life to cause you to feel different about love. If love caused this deep pain, then perhaps love is responsible for the beauty in your life because it's been repressed and hidden until now.

5. Your old beliefs of love will be challenged if your soul is unprepared to learn about life. Your twin flame is likely to be someone you fear may have already experienced love that you haven't.

6. You'll know when the time is right for a twin flame relationship; your intuition will tell you.

7. If you want a twin flame relationship, consider changing your life by letting go of certain things or people holding you back. It could mean eliminating certain friends or family members, taking on a new career, moving to another place, or changing how you spend your time and money.

8. It's possible to find your twin flame, but you have to make room for them in your life. Set aside the time, energy, and resources for them, and allow yourself to feel the love you've been holding back.

9. Your twin flame didn't come into your life by accident. They are there to help you overcome your fears about love and teach you about unconditional love and relationships, meaning they'll be there when you least expect them for this teaching to happen.

10. Love is the most important thing in life, and it's the only thing that gives meaning to our existence on this planet. If you've been looking for love, you've likely been looking for your twin flame because they're one and the same. Your twin flame will teach you how to find love and give it unconditionally.

Quiz: Am I with My Twin Flame?

1. Do you often feel that time stands still with them?
2. Do you have dreams about them that come true the next day?
3. When you first met them, did they seem familiar?
4. Do you feel like you have known them from another lifetime?

5. Do you feel that you have special psychic or spiritual powers in common with them?

6. Do you think about them constantly, even when they're not physically present?

7. Does it seem like your life and everyone else's lives revolve around you?

8. Do they finish your sentences or what you're thinking?

9. Do you feel your whole world is turned upside down when you are physically separated from them?

10. Do you feel like they bring out the best in you and improve your life?

If you answered yes to six or more of these questions, congratulations!. You've got your twin flame.

Chapter 9: A Guide to Soul Mates

What is the difference between twin flames and soul mates? What are soul mates like? What does it mean to find your soul mate? There's a lot of confusion around the concept of "soul mates," so let's clear that right up. Twin flames are two halves of a soul chosen to incarnate into a lifetime in two bodies. On the other hand, soul mates are two separate souls sharing an instant connection upon meeting, and this connection may or may not be romantic.

Soul Mates and Astrology

If you want your soul mate relationships to work, it's worth looking at the natal charts of both people involved to determine how the planets affect you both and how to dance with this person to create magic and love between you. While soul mate relationships and friendships can work without the knowledge of the planetary placements, it's worth looking at the charts to make these connections even more divine and fulfilling for everyone involved.

Signs You've Met Your Soul Mate

You sense their presence before you even see them: Other people around you notice this too, but they don't understand why. Your heart skips a beat when you first lay eyes on them. When they walk into the room and your eyes meet, you get butterflies in your stomach. You may feel nauseous and experience other physical changes in your body when they're around. This is called "love at first sight," and it's very common in soul mate relationships. The next time this happens, pay attention to what's happening right then and there because the Universe is telling you this person is your soul mate.

You feel like you've known them forever: There's no awkwardness or hesitation when you talk to each other, and you instantly feel you could tell this person anything about yourself and know they won't judge you. You feel that talking to this person is as natural as talking to an old friend or family member because, on some level, they are an old friend or family member.

You and your soul mate want the same things in life: This is where thorough astrological compatibility comes in handy. If you both have the same moon sign or have other planets in the same signs, you're bound to have similar goals and ideas about approaching your life together. It is a good thing because the more you can work together to achieve your shared goals, the more aligned you'll be in life - soul mates often feel they've known each other their entire lives.

You feel whole when you're together: When you're with your soul mate, you feel that every part of yourself has reached its full potential and purpose. Your soul mate fills a part of you that was missing or missing something, making an instant connection between you.

You have the same philosophy of life: Perhaps you feel there's one overriding theme running through your entire life as you come to understand what it means to be a soul mate. You feel that together you can bring this theme into being. With two brains working together, your goals can become even more powerful and effective than if focusing individually on your end goals in life.

You know when the other person is lying or telling the truth: On some level, you can see past their layers, read the emotions behind their eyes, sense the energies flowing between you, and see things no one else would notice. You may even share telepathy.

The Pros of a Soul Mate Relationship

Soul mate relationships are very rewarding. Soul mate relationships are some of the most fulfilling, magical, and loving relationships you can have on Earth. They're relationship goals many people choose to pursue in their lifetimes and come with the promise that once you've found your soul mate, the rest of your life will fall into place in a very beautiful way. You'll feel loved and adored like no one else can feel or give to you.

As soul mates, you have a deeper connection than most other people. When you meet your soul mate, you will feel an instant connection that is incredible, profound, and can only be described as unity and wholeness. You will feel you are one person with different bodies and minds operating simultaneously. You'll know things about each other no one else knows because you share the same consciousness or mind on some level.

Being a soul mate gives you deeper insight into people around you. The closer a soul mate relationship gets, the more you will understand the other person, and the better you can help them with their problems. You'll also feel an overwhelming sense of love and compassion for them when they need it most, and that's one of the best things you can do for a friend in need.

Your soul mate will always support your dreams. On some level, they feel they're your dreams as well. Your goals are their goals because they want you to succeed as much as you do. They'll give you all the support you need to get there.

Having a soul mate makes you feel more fulfilled and content. You may even find yourself working better in your career and life because of your deep connection with your soul mate. You'll feel you have a purpose and everything in the world makes sense to you now, and there's nothing left to do except enjoy your time with this person who is meant for you.

Your soul mate will help you heal whatever pain or past trauma weighs on your heart. Your soul mate will make you feel you're the most special and important person in the world. Whether or not your soul mate knows this is true, they will give you all of the love, attention, and care you need to heal from the pain or regrets holding you back.

The Cons of a Soul Mate Relationship

Soul mate relationships aren't always easy, and they don't come with a lifetime guarantee. Sometimes soul mates go through rough patches or differences of opinion on how to approach life. Sometimes you'll disagree on how to handle your children or deal with your extended families, etc. It doesn't mean you aren't soul mates. It only means you're going through an adjustment period and learning how to deal with each other.

Your soul mate doesn't always have the same feelings about you. If your soul mate has had a rough past, they may not have learned to love unconditionally, which is the foundation of a soul mate relationship. Due to this, they cannot truly see your strengths and all you have to offer, and also, you cannot see some of their weaknesses.

Soul mates sometimes cause each other more problems than they're worth. Probably the most common problem with soul mates, but definitely not the only one – plenty more issues can arise, jealousy or problems with family members, etc.

Soul mates can drive each other crazy. Even though you feel enormous love and joy when you're in a soul mate relationship, it can sometimes be hard on your partner. Soul mates might get jealous or depressed when they aren't getting the attention they crave from one another.

Soul mates can sometimes lead each other down the wrong path. If you've previously been in a soul mate relationship, you could use your next relationship merely as a crutch in your desire for validation and love.

Soul mates often get away with things they shouldn't. Due to your deep connection, it isn't easy to see the harm they're doing to others because personal information about both of you will now be revealed.

Challenges in a Soul Mate Relationship

Soul mates sometimes want to control each other. This happens if one soul mate feels they need to protect the other from making mistakes or causing themselves any degree of harm. If this happens, talk it out and make sure you're not becoming overly controlling with each other.

Soul mates are prone to cheating. Soul mate relationships are very passionate and exciting on the surface level, so cheating could be an issue. It can be resolved by talking about your problems and ensuring you're being 100 percent honest with one another.

Soul mates are sometimes selfish. This is another problem common in soul mate relationships because you spend much more time together and think you can get away with more. It's important always to be honest with each other and do things out of love rather than selfishness to make sure this doesn't become a chronic issue.

Soul mates sometimes only see the flaws in one another. This happens when your partner distances themselves and withdraws their love from the relationship because of past trauma or hard life experiences. It's important to work through your problems together and that you don't neglect or ignore the good things your partner does.

Soul mates are sometimes jealous of each other. Not all soul mates are created equal – some are more jealous than others, and it is a problem in many ways if not addressed. If your partner is jealous of you, make sure you're not doing or saying anything you wouldn't want your partner to do or say about you. Remember, you are both human and deserve to be loved without judgment.

Soul mates are sometimes complacent with their relationship. This is especially true when you're used to being around each other all the time and don't get enough attention or affection from your soul mate. Remind one another why you fell in love. Renew the passion by talking about your goals and dreams and how they relate to both of you.

Advice for Being in a Soul Mate Relationship

1. Always be completely honest with one another. Lies are a death sentence because nobody can have a truly authentic connection with someone who is deliberately lying.

2. Make sure that your partner is happy and sure of the relationship.

3. Don't get jealous. Jealousy is a huge turn-off and clouds judgment, so embrace your selfishness as often as possible because it's a major source of strength and could make up for shortcomings on the other end of the spectrum.

4. Make sure that you're not expecting your partner to be perfect. People are not perfect, so never expect your soul mate to be any different. If you have a problem with something they're doing, let them know immediately, rather than sitting and dwelling on it due to your fears or insecurities.

5. Never take advantage of one another. It is a major issue that will only lead to more problems and frustration in the long run.

6. It's essential never to put each other down to make yourself look better.

7. You are not the bigger person in any given situation, especially if your partner is being the bigger person and doing something for you out of love.

8. Make sure you are not constantly putting off real-life responsibilities because of your soul mate.

Advice for Finding Your Soul Mate

1. Look beyond physical appearances and ask yourself who you're truly attracted to.

217

2. Ask yourself what you're most attracted to about a person.

3. Admire people for their positive qualities, not only the ones you feel will be the most beneficial to your relationship.

4. Stay optimistic and avoid being too critical or judgmental of other people.

5. Pay attention to your intuition, and don't force yourself to be with someone who does not feel they're the right one for you.

6. Make sure that you're not attracted to someone purely because you share the same interests.

7. Don't be afraid of changing your mind about someone if you really think it's the right thing to do.

8. Don't be afraid of taking risks in a relationship because no soul mate will come knocking on your door or fall from the sky if you don't open yourself up to the possibility of meeting new people.

9. Be yourself and let others be themselves, too. Avoid pushing them away or distancing yourself from them because they don't perfectly match your ideals.

10. If you can't be yourself 10o percent of the time and are still in a relationship with your soul mate, perhaps that relationship isn't what you truly want.

Quiz: Am I with My Soul Mate?

1. Do you feel like you could never get tired of being with your partner?

2. Are they always willing to do whatever it takes to make sure you remain in close contact?

3. Are you able to talk about anything and everything with your partner for hours on end? Do you enjoy doing this together?

4. Does your partner love you for who you are and not what they want to make out of you due to their selfish desires?

5. Does your mate make you feel like you're the only person in the entire world for them?

6. Are your days and nights filled with so much passion you feel your life is perfect?

7. Do you feel like your partner has a purpose in your life?

8. Do they make you feel important and special?

9. Do they inspire you to be a better person?

10. Do you find their words and actions congruent with each other?

If you answered yes to 6 or more of these questions, congratulations! You've got a soul mate.

Chapter 10: Spiritual Well-Being 101

What is spiritual well-being? It's the feeling of peace and contentment, self-acceptance, and value a person experiences when they know their worth. It happens when people fully accept themselves and take what they need. You can easily overcome sadness, anger, or anxiety by learning about your emotions and accepting what they're designed to teach you.

The Connection between Spiritual Astrology and Spiritual Well-Being

Spiritual astrology is a tool meant to help us accomplish the state of spiritual well-being, where we're embodying our true selves and accomplishing our life mission. If you want to experience true spiritual well-being, you'd be hard-pressed to find a better way than looking at your astrological chart and learning the planets and their energies that will help you rise to the level you belong in life.

Why You Should Take Your Spiritual Health Seriously

Many people today don't take their spiritual health seriously. They aren't living a purposeful life and not accomplishing what they meant to do in this lifetime. You may be one of those people, and that's okay, but don't let it get you down. Astrology will help you benefit from your birth chart and achieve the life you deserve.

Your spiritual health is important if you want to experience wholesome relationships. Why should you care? Because you'll walk through life with a greater awareness of who you are and what your life is about. Your life will be surrounded by meaningful, like-minded people making it more enjoyable and comfortable.

Your Purpose, Authentic Self, and Spiritual Well-Being

You can't live a purposeful life without knowing who you are. You'll make the most of your unique experience and feel comfortable in your skin. Your spiritual well-being is improved when you accept who you are and understand we're all connected as one being in this world. When you're willing to listen to your inner self, your life will become more meaningful, and your relationships will become more satisfying.

Practices You Can Use to Improve Your Spiritual Well-Being

Allow yourself to confront your emotions. If you're feeling angry, sad, or resentful, look at yourself and see how you feel. You're likely feeling a little uncomfortable about something, and if you can identify it, you can work through it. If you cannot understand how to improve your spiritual well-being, practice confronting the issue openly. Talk to someone to determine what's happening to you so that you can make the necessary changes in yourself.

Accept the negative emotions that arise in your life. Sometimes, it's necessary to feel anxiety or anger. Sometimes, these emotions teach us about ourselves. If you can learn to be comfortable with your emotions, they won't hold you back or get in the way of your life purpose.

Enjoy the world around you and make the most of your surroundings. The easiest way to experience spiritual well-being is to surround yourself with people you love, enjoy spending time with, and have meaningful conversations about life and its purpose. If you live your life creatively or compassionately, you'll grow stronger and stronger in yourself.

Do things that take you out of your comfort zone. When you're constantly comfortable, it's hard to feel new emotions or experiences. If you want to experience new things, make an effort to get out of your comfort zone and do something new. The more challenging the experience, the more likely you feel a deeper level of connection with yourself and the world.

Get rid of negative people from your life who don't support your spiritual health journey. If someone consistently challenges you, makes you feel bad about yourself, or otherwise brings your spirits down, it is time to let them go. Letting go of these people doesn't mean you're ungrateful for their help or aren't good friends. It means you've grown enough as a human and spiritual being to know when certain relationships no longer serve your purpose.

Develop a sense of humor about life and yourself. If you can learn to laugh at the little things in life and yourself, you'll develop more confidence as a spiritual being and an authentic self. If you can feel comfortable with yourself, you'll experience a deeper sense of well-being, making you more confident in your everyday life.

Take life seriously, but not yourself. It's okay to take your life seriously, but it's not okay to take yourself too seriously. Give yourself leeway to understand why things happen, and being more laid back will help you as an individual and spiritually.

Meditate for at least 5 to 10 minutes every day. You don't have to meditate for hours for it to be effective. Taking a few minutes out of your day can make a big difference in your life. The more frequently you meditate, the easier it is to recognize your emotions and understand where they came from and how they relate to your experiences as an authentic self and spiritual being.

Practice self-forgiveness. For many people, there's nothing easier than beating themselves up over something that happened in the past or something they did wrong along their life journey. If this is an issue in your life, you must be more forgiving of yourself. It's valuable to recognize that we all make mistakes, but it's important to learn to enjoy what you do right to preserve your authenticity and purpose.

Practice self-acceptance. You need to accept yourself for who you are to experience spiritual well-being. If you don't accept what your life has been until now, it will be difficult to accept yourself as a person capable of making the necessary changes the right way at the right time.

Signs of High Spiritual Well-Being

When you're practicing these spiritual well-being techniques, you'll notice big changes in your life. Here are a few:

Your mood improves. If you're feeling happier and more positive about yourself and the people around you, your spiritual well-being is likely improving. When you take the time to feel good about who you are and where your life path is, anxiety or depression will fade.

You develop empathy for yourself and others. When your spiritual well-being is high, you'll empathize with people going through difficult times. You recognize the emotions people are experiencing, making it easier to understand their feelings and needs and provide them assistance.

You're more open. When you feel good about yourself and the people around you, it's easier to open up to situations and new people to expand your circle of trust and friendship. If these connections help bring out more of yourself than they take away, they positively contribute to your emotional well-being.

You're more creative. Many people feel that a spiritual connection helps them be more creative, insightful, and ultimately more in touch with their intuition. When your intuition is strong and your creativity is flourishing, you feel spiritually well because you discover many ways of expressing yourself.

You see things differently. When you've grown stronger as a spiritual being, your entire perspective on life can change. You'll see beyond the limits of what life previously gave you and learn to live a much stronger and happier life as an authentic self with nothing holding them back.

Spiritual Well-Being in Your Relationship

The following are some of the ways that these techniques will develop trust, respect, and affection in your relationship:

1. You have better communication and listening skills.
2. You recognize your partner's emotions at any given moment.
3. You understand what circumstances make your partner feel good about themselves and their lives and what circumstances make them doubtful or worried.
4. When appropriate, you offer suggestions or advice on how they could make things better for themselves.

5. You become more empathetic to your partner's struggles.

Spiritual Well-Being at Home

A strong sense of spiritual well-being improves the atmosphere at home. Here are some ways it can be achieved:

1. You tolerate difficult situations with less anxiety.
2. You appreciate the small things that make your life more enjoyable, like a good cup of coffee or a massage.
3. You accept your partner or family members for who they are and where they're at in their lives.
4. You have better relationships with your partner or family members for communicating how you feel about certain situations and how to resolve them effectively.
5. You understand other people's needs and recognize that you can offer assistance during situations when necessary and appropriate.

Spiritual Well-Being at the Workplace

Here's what spiritual well-being looks like in the workplace:

1. You enjoy the benefits of a good work-life balance.
2. You embrace the creativity to express yourself at work and use it to find new opportunities for growth and development in your career.
3. You communicate with your coworkers clearly and respectfully, helping you work diligently without getting bogged down in drama or politics.
4. You're less anxious and stressed dealing with difficult situations at work or with other people in the office.
5. You know you are growing and thriving as a person, which ultimately helps you do better work every day because you're more confident about your abilities.

Spiritual Well-Being in Society

When societal well-being is high, you feel good about the world because you feel your country, state, or community is taken care of instead of being abused. Here are a few ways that spiritual well-being affects society positively:

1. You have an overall sense of peace and contentment with your surroundings.
2. You feel there is less violence and conflict in your community and country than in other areas of the world.
3. You understand people need help when they're going through a hard time – and treat them with more kindness and respect.
4. You feel more connected with other people in your community, which helps you feel safer and more secure.
5. When your spiritual well-being is high, you want to take better care of yourself and others to show gratitude for what you have in life.

These are merely a few ways spiritual well-being can improve your life when used with a healthy dose of mindfulness and gratitude.

Quiz: How High Is My Spiritual Well-Being?

Answer yes or no to the following:
1. I feel I have a purpose in life.
2. I can easily recall past events that were meaningful to me or had a positive effect on my life.
3. I attempt to make something of my life every day by working hard, learning new things, or exploring different opportunities for growth and development.
4. I understand other people's feelings or points of view, even if we disagree about a situation or about what is important in life.
5. I feel the world around me is a safe place to live in.
6. I feel I have support from other people in tough situations.
7. I'm supportive of people when they're going through a difficult time.
8. I respect other people's views, opinions, and ideas, even if they don't coincide with my beliefs.
9. I feel that the work I do is good because it's more fulfilling or meaningful to me personally than anything else.
10. I feel I can communicate with my partner or family members so they appreciate how I feel, without causing an argument, or bringing up negative feelings.

11. I tolerate difficult situations, knowing that everything will be okay regardless of what happens in life.

12. I have good relationships with my colleagues at work, even if we don't necessarily see eye-to-eye on certain things.

13. I desire to help people in the world because it makes me happy to see them get ahead and succeed.

14. I enjoy my successes without feeling arrogant or superior toward other people.

15. I am myself around people who don't necessarily agree with my way of seeing things or what I want from life.

16. I don't feel the need to always be right or correct people when they do or say something I disagree with.

17. When I see negative situations on the news, I feel compassion for other people and offer assistance if needed.

18. I feel I can make a positive difference in the world by doing what I'm good at, not necessarily because of money or success.

19. I have the ability to correct toxic problems in my life so that they don't continue to haunt me.

20. I have a strong desire to help people find their inner peace, whatever that means to them.

If you answered yes to 14 questions or more, you're doing great with your spiritual well-being.

Bonus: Guide to Refuel Your Spiritual Well-Being

Here's a 30-day guide to healing yourself spiritually.

Day 1: Go for a walk outside.

Day 2: Meditate for ten minutes in the morning.

Day 3: Write down the things that matter the most to you in a journal.

Day 4: Do something kind for someone, but make it someone who can't pay you back.

Day 5: Buy something nice for yourself.

Day 6: Look in the mirror and affirm, "You're doing great. I love you," for five minutes.

Day 7: Three times today, stop whatever you're doing and smile for one minute.

Day 8: Spend time with someone you enjoy being with. Just be there for them.

Day 9: Listen to an empowering podcast.

Day 10: Prepare yourself a healthy, sumptuous meal.

Day 11: Find a way to spend time with your favorite animal.

Day 12: For five minutes, dance to your favorite song.

Day 13: Journal for five minutes about your flaws. Do this with no judgment, only love.

Day 14: Journal for five minutes about your best qualities and bask in them.

Day 15: Donate something to a cause that matters to you.

Day 16: Ask anyone around you if there's something you can help with.

Day 17: Meditate for ten minutes before bed.

Day 18: Write down ten things that you're thankful for.

Day 19: Write down five things you love about the person dearest to you.

Day 20: Dress up sharp and beautifully.

Day 21: Spend five minutes journaling about your progress in life.

Day 22: Have fun at the park or in your yard without your phone for an hour.

Day 23: Meditate for fifteen minutes in the morning.

Day 24: Write down five things you know you need to stop doing. Pick one and end it.

Day 25: Make a list of the toxic people in your life. Pick one and cut them out of your life.

Day 26: Work out for five to ten minutes and be present and feel your body.

Day 27: Stay off social media.

Day 28: Pay attention to your water intake, and stay hydrated.

Day 29: Meditate on all the good things in your life, and feel deep appreciation for them. Do this for ten minutes.

Day 30: when you eat, be more mindful and present. Pay attention to the colors, smells, and textures as you eat.

Here's another book by Mari Silva that you might like

Your Free Gift
(only available for a limited time)

Thanks for getting this book! If you want to learn more about various spirituality topics, then join Mari Silva's community and get a free guided meditation MP3 for awakening your third eye. This guided meditation mp3 is designed to open and strengthen ones third eye so you can experience a higher state of consciousness. Simply visit the link below the image to get started.

https://spiritualityspot.com/meditation

Or, Scan the QR code!

Bibliography

A, S. (2019, May 29). *Karmic astrology: Know your karma and your dharma.* WeMystic. https://www.wemystic.com/karmic-astrology/

Admin. (2013, December 12). *Karmic astrology.* ZodiacSign.com. https://www.sunsigns.org/karmic-astrology/

Allard, S. (2020, September 4). *5 things to know about karma and reincarnation.* Hindu American Foundation. https://www.hinduamerican.org/blog/5-things-to-know-about-karma-and-reincarnation

Astrology.Com. (n.d). *Birth chart calculator.* Accessed October 1, 2022. https://www.astrology.com/birth-chart/

Astrology Zodiac Signs. (n.d.). *Karmic astrology.* Astrology-Zodiac-Signs.Com. Accessed October 1, 2022. https://www.astrology-zodiac-signs.com/astrology/branches/karmic-astrology/

AstroTwins. (2020, August 31). *12 houses of the horoscope: The themes & lessons of each.* Mindbodygreen. https://www.mindbodygreen.com/articles/the-12-houses-of-astrology/

AstroTwins. (2019, June 30). *Create your free birth chart.* Astrostyle. https://astrostyle.com/birthchart/?sscid=51k6_wugvp

AstroTwins. (2019, January 31). *How to read your birth chart like an astrologer.* Mindbodygreen. https://www.mindbodygreen.com/articles/how-to-read-your-astrology-birth-chart/

Black, K. M. (n.d.). *Karmic astrology: The secret to a happy, purposeful life.* Karen M. Black. Accessed October 1, 2022. https://www.karenmblack.com/karmic-astrology.html

Black, K. M (n.d.). *Your north node soul mission: Detailed descriptions by sign and house.* Karen M. Black. Accessed October 1, 2022.

https://www.karenmblack.com/north-node.html

Cafe Astrology .com. (2018, March 15). *Understanding the astrological chart wheel.* https://cafeastrology.com/articles/how-to-understand-read-chart-wheel.html

Camacho, N. A. (2022, May 18). *What the astrological house associated with your zodiac sign means for you.* Well+Good. https://www.wellandgood.com/zodiac-signs-houses/

Dasa, P. (2014, October 8). *Reincarnation and karma: How it all works.* HuffPost.

Discover Card. (2014, September 17). *How good is your karma?* BuzzFeed. https://www.buzzfeed.com/discovercard/how-good-is-your-karma

Estrada, J. (2022, June 28). *There are 12 laws of karma at play in your life—here's what they mean.* Well+Good. https://www.wellandgood.com/12-laws-of-karma/

Estrela, A. (2019, November 6). *Forecasting the future.* PsychicGuild. https://www.psychicguild.com/astrology/forecasting/

Harra, C. (2020, February 21). *5 ways karma from your past lives affects you today.* Mindbodygreen. https://www.mindbodygreen.com/0-20223/5-ways-karma-from-your-past-lives-affects-you-today.html

Heyl, J. C. (2022, March 24). *What is a karmic cycle?* Dotdash Media. https://www.verywellmind.com/what-is-a-karmic-cycle-5219446

Hinduism Today. (2019, September 5). *Karma and reincarnation.* https://www.hinduismtoday.com/hindu-basics/karma-and-reincarnation/

Hope grows. (2020, April 24). *What is spiritual purpose?* https://hopegrows.net/news/what-is-spiritual-purpose

Kauai's Hindu Monastery. (n.d.). *Basics of Hinduism.* Accessed October 1, 2022. https://www.himalayanacademy.com/readlearn/basics/karma-reincarnation

Kelly, A. (2022, November 30). *12 zodiac signs: Dates and personality traits of each star sign.* Allure. https://www.allure.com/story/zodiac-sign-personality-traits-dates

Kelly, A. (2021, July 4). *Birth charts 101: Understanding the planets and their meanings.* Allure. https://www.allure.com/story/astrology-birth-chart-reading

Kelly, A. (2021, June 8). *What houses in your birth chart mean and how to find them.* Allure. https://www.allure.com/story/12-astrology-houses-meaning

Kent, A. E. (2015). *Astrological transits: The beginner's guide to using planetary cycles to plan and predict your day, week, year (or destiny).* Fair Winds Press.

LaMeaux, E. C. (n.d.). *How to attract good karma.* Gaiam. https://www.gaiam.com/blogs/discover/how-to-attract-good-karma

Leek, S. (1977). *Moon signs.* W.H. Allen/Virgin Books.

Lindberg, S. (2020, November 5). *What are the 12 laws of karma?* Healthline Media. https://www.healthline.com/health/laws-of-karma

Lynsreadings.com. (n.d.). *Frequency of numbers and karmic lessons.* Accessed October 1, 2022. https://www.lynsreadings.com/karmic-lessons

Magner, E. (2022, October 4). *12 houses in astrology: Understand a new level of your zodiac sign.* Well+Good. https://www.wellandgood.com/houses-in-astrology/

Moses. (2021, March 17). *6 signs you're experiencing a karmic lesson.* PsychDigital.

Murphy, B., Jr. (2015, March 11). *10 selfless ways to build good karma and generate happiness.* Inc. Australia. https://www.inc.com/bill-murphy-jr/10-selfless-ways-to-build-good-karma-and-generate-happiness.html

Penix, S. (2018, July 9). *How the law of karmic return can help you be a better person.* Study Breaks. https://studybreaks.com/thoughts/karmic-return/

Regan, S. (2020, July 17). *How to recognize a karmic lesson & what to do about it.* Mindbodygreen. https://www.mindbodygreen.com/articles/signs-youre-receiving-a-karmic-lesson-and-what-to-do-about-it/

Regan, S. (2021, May 19). *What actually is karmic debt & how can you know if you have it?* Mindbodygreen. https://www.mindbodygreen.com/articles/karmic-debt/

Schulman, M. (1977). *Karmic astrology: v. 1.* HarperCollins Distribution Services.

Stardust, L. (2021, March 30). *How to read your birth chart.* Teen Vogue. https://www.teenvogue.com/story/how-to-read-your-birth-chart

Stinson, N. (2017, December 15). *10 ways to align with your purpose or dharma.* Chopra. https://chopra.com/articles/10-ways-to-align-with-your-purpose-or-dharma

Summit Publications. (2013, April 3). *35. The law of karmic return.* https://www.summitlighthouse.org/inner-perspectives/karma-law-of-karmic-return/

Thomas, K. (2022, January 27). *What is a birth chart in astrology — and how do you read one?* New York Post. https://nypost.com/article/astrology-birth-chart/

TrustedTeller. (2021, December 14). *Understanding zodiac signs: Elements, qualities, and polarity.* https://trustedteller.com/blog/understanding-zodiac-signs-elements-qualities-and-polarity/

Vedanta Society of Southern California. (2016, March 14). *Karma and reincarnation.* https://vedanta.org/what-is-vedanta/karma-and-reincarnation/

Wehrstein, K. M. "Reincarnation and karma." *Psi Encyclopedia* (2021, July 7.). https://psi-encyclopedia.spr.ac.uk/articles/reincarnation-and-karma

Whitney, B. (2017, June 15). How's your karma? Zoo. https://www.zoo.com/quiz/hows-your-karma

Wright, J. (2022, March 18). *There are (at least) 9 types of astrology—which one's right for you?* PureWow. https://www.purewow.com/wellness/types-of-astrology

ZodiacPsychics.com. (n.d.). *What is karmic astrology?* Accessed October 1, 2022. https://www.zodiacpsychics.com/article/what-is-karmic-astrology.html

Bailey, A. A., & Khul, D. (1997). Esoteric astrology (Vol. 3). Lucis Publishing Companies.

Barton, T. (2002). Ancient astrology. Routledge.

Campion, Nicholas (1982). An Introduction to the History of Astrology. ISCWA.

Campion, Nicholas (2008). A History of Western Astrology. The Ancient World (vol. 1). London Continuum.

Holden, James Herschel (2006). A History of Horoscopic Astrology (2nd ed.). AFA.

Kay, Richard (1994). Dante's Christian Astrology. Middle Ages Series. University of Pennsylvania Press.

Newman, W. R., Grafton, A., & Viano, C. (2006). Secrets of nature: astrology and alchemy in early modern Europe. Aestimatio: Critical Reviews in the History of Science.

Parker, Derek; Parker, Julia (1983). A history of astrology. Deutsch.

Robbins, Frank E., ed. (1940). Ptolemy Tetrabiblos. Harvard University Press (Loeb Classical Library).

Tester, S. J. (1987). A history of western astrology. Boydell & Brewer.

Veenstra, J.R. (1997). Magic and Divination at the Courts of Burgundy and France: Text and Context of Laurens Pignon's "Contre les Devineurs" (1411). Brill.

Wedel, Theodore Otto (1920). The Medieval Attitude Toward Astrology: Particularly in England. Yale University Press.

Wood, Chauncey (1970). Chaucer and the Country of the Stars: Poetical Uses of Astrological Imagery. Princeton University Press

Printed in Great Britain
by Amazon

58084844R00137